The Constitution of the United States

A LOOK AT THE SECOND AMENDMENT

TO KEEP AND BEAR ARMS

DOREEN GONZALES

MyReportLinks.com Books
an imprint of

Enslow Publishers, Inc.
Box 398, 40 Industrial Road
Berkeley Heights, NJ 07922
USA

MyReportLinks.com Books, an imprint of Enslow Publishers, Inc. MyReportLinks®
is a registered trademark of Enslow Publishers, Inc.

Library of Congress Cataloging-in-Publication Data

Gonzales, Doreen.
  A look at the Second Amendment : to keep and bear arms / Doreen Gonzales.
    p. cm. — (The Constitution of the United States)
  Includes bibliographical references and index.
  ISBN-13: 978-1-59845-061-3
  ISBN-10: 1-59845-061-1
  1. United States. Constitution. 2nd Amendment—History—Juvenile literature. 2. Firearms—Law and
legislation—United States—Juvenile literature. 3. Gun control—United States—Juvenile literature. 4.
Firearms ownership—Government policy—United States—Juvenile literature. [1. United States.
Constitution. 2nd Amendment—History. 2. Firearms—Law and legislation—United States. 3. Gun con-
trol—United States. 4. Firearms ownership—Government policy—United States.] I. Title.
  KF3941.G64 2008
  344.7305'33—dc22

                                        2006022411

Printed in the United States of America

10 9 8 7 6 5 4 3 2 1

To Our Readers:
Through the purchase of this book, you and your library gain access to the Report Links that specifically
back up this book.
The Publisher will provide access to the Report Links that back up this book and will keep these Report
Links up to date on **www.myreportlinks.com** for five years from the book's first publication date.
We have done our best to make sure all Internet addresses in this book were active and appropriate when
we went to press. However, the author and the Publisher have no control over, and assume no liability
for, the material available on those Internet sites or on other Web sites they may link to.
The usage of the MyReportLinks.com Books Web site is subject to the terms and conditions stated on the
Usage Policy Statement on **www.myreportlinks.com.**
A password may be required to access the Report Links that back up this book. The password is found
on the bottom of page 4 of this book.
Any comments or suggestions can be sent by e-mail to comments@myreportlinks.com or to the address
on the back cover.

CONTENTS

MyReportLinks.com Books
Great Books, Great Links, Great for Research!

The Internet sites featured in this book can save you hours of research time. These Internet sites—we call them **"Report Links"**—are constantly changing, but we keep them up to date on our Web site.

When you see this "Approved Web Site" logo, you will know that we are directing you to a great Internet site that will help you with your research.

Give it a try! Type http://www.myreportlinks.com into your browser, click on the series title and enter the password, then click on the book title, and scroll down to the Report Links listed for this book.

The Report Links will bring you to great source documents, photographs, and illustrations. MyReportLinks.com Books save you time, feature Report Links that are kept up to date, and make report writing easier than ever! A complete listing of the Report Links can be found on pages 116–117 at the back of the book.

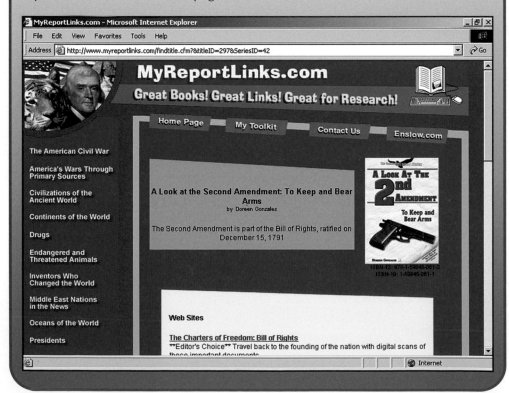

Please see "To Our Readers" on the copyright page for important information about this book, the MyReportLinks.com Web site, and the Report Links that back up this book.

Please enter **SAC1956** if asked for a password.

TIME LINE

1770— British soldiers kill five unarmed Boston colonists. This becomes known as the Boston Massacre.

1775— American colonists and Minutemen turn back British forces at Concord, Massachusetts. Colonial leaders create the Continental Army. George Washington is named its commander. The Revolutionary War begins. In the beginning, it is fought by the Continental Army and colonial militias.

1783— The Revolutionary War officially ends, making the United States of America a new nation.

1791— The Bill of Rights is added to the United States Constitution. It includes the Second Amendment. The wording of the amendment will lead to disagreements about its meaning. Some people will hold that the amendment protects every person's right to own a firearm. Others will say that it only protects a state's right to organize military groups.

1792— The Militia Act is passed. It requires all white men between the ages of eighteen and forty-five to serve in a militia.

1822— The case of *Bliss* v. *Kentucky* upholds an individual's right to bear arms in the state of Kentucky.

1833— In *Barron* v. *Baltimore,* the Supreme Court rules that the Constitution protects people from the actions of the federal government. This means that the Second Amendment only applies to laws written by the federal government.

1846— In a Georgia court, the case of *Nunn* v. *Georgia* reaffirms an individual's right to bear arms. It does, however, uphold a state's right to place some restrictions on this right.

1868— The Fourteenth Amendment is passed after the Civil War to give African Americans equal rights. The amendment prohibits states from taking away any citizen's fundamental rights.

1876— The Supreme Court rules in *Presser* v. *Illinois* that while states may not ban individuals from having a firearm, they may regulate military bodies.

1903— The U.S. Congress passes the Dick Act. Its purpose is to strengthen the state militias.

1917— Many state militias are drafted to fight in World War I.

1933— All state militias are officially renamed National Guards. The National Guard becomes a part of the U.S. Army.

1934— The National Firearms Act restricts ownership of automatic weapons and sawed-off shotguns.

1938— The Federal Firearms Act is passed. It requires some gun dealers to have a Federal Firearms License. It also requires that dealers keep records of who purchases their guns. Finally, it outlaws the selling of guns to convicted felons.

1939— In *U.S.* v. *Miller,* the Supreme Court issues a collective rights ruling of the Second Amendment. It says the Second Amendment was written to guarantee states the right to form their own military units. This ruling says that the amendment only gives individuals the right to own guns for use in a government-sponsored army.

TIME LINE (CONT.)

1942— In *Cases* v. *U.S.* the Supreme Court upholds the collective rights theory of gun ownership. The Court says that federal laws can regulate individual gun ownership.

1968— The Omnibus Crime Control Act is passed. Its laws restrict certain types of guns, gun ownership, and gun dealers. The same year the Supreme Court refuses to hear the case of *Burton* v. *Sills.* In effect, this refusal allows states to regulate individual gun ownership.

1982— The Supreme Court refuses to hear another case about state gun laws. Again, by not hearing *Quilici* v. *Village of Morton Grove,* the Supreme Court upholds a state's right to regulate guns.

1986— Passage of the McClure-Volkmer Act eases restrictions on gun dealers.

1993— The Brady Handgun Violence Prevention Act is passed. It requires a five-day waiting period for anyone wanting to buy a gun. Also this year, federal authorities storm the headquarters of a religious cult called the Branch Davidians. The Davidians are known to have weapons and are suspected of abusing their members. Eighty Davidians and four federal agents are killed in the encounter.

1994— Passage of the Assault Weapons Ban outlaws several kinds of semiautomatic weapons.

1995— The Supreme Court rules in *U.S.* v. *Lopez* that the U.S. Congress cannot outlaw guns in school zones. This, it says, is a matter for each state.

1997— In *Kitchen* v. *K-Mart Corporation,* the Florida Supreme Court holds the K-Mart Corporation responsible for damage caused when one of its employees sells a gun to an intoxicated person.

1998— The five-day waiting period for buying a gun is replaced. A new computerized system now checks to see if a gun buyer is a criminal. It is called the National Instant Criminal Background Check System (NICS).

1999— Twelve students and one teacher are killed with assault weapons at Columbine High School in Littleton, Colorado. The two students who commit the crime then kill themselves.

2001— In *U.S.* v. *Emerson,* the Supreme Court again upholds the collective rights view of the Second Amendment. It rules that a state can restrict guns from certain individuals. In September of this year, the United States is attacked by a terrorist organization called al-Qaeda. This raises concerns about terrorists obtaining weapons in the United States.

2004— The Assault Weapons Ban expires. Congress does not renew it.

2006— Controversy over the meaning of the Second Amendment continues. At one extreme are people who believe the amendment protects an individual's right to own a gun. At the other extreme are those who think the amendment is about a state's right to have an armed military organization. They believe the amendment says nothing about personal ownership. Groups of varying opinions continue to work with Congress to have their opinions heard and put into law.

THE SECOND AMENDMENT TODAY

hen Sandra Phillips stepped out of her home one morning in 2006, an attacker was waiting for her. He was dressed in black and was wearing a mask. He was also holding a gun. The man grabbed Phillips, but she jerked free and ran back into her house. The attacker followed.

Mrs. Phillips screamed to her husband who was sleeping in the bedroom. He woke up, grabbed his revolver, and ran to his wife. When he reached her, the intruder had his arm around her neck and a gun in his hand. Mr. Louis John Phillips took careful aim and shot the intruder, David Edward Ferguson.

Ferguson, though, was not dead. He turned toward Mr. Phillips, without letting go of Sandra. Mr. Phillips then shot his gun two more times. Both shots hit Ferguson, and he finally fell to the floor and died.[1]

Having a gun close by may have saved the Phillips's lives. The police later found Ferguson had been carrying a knife and BB handgun. He also had a piece of rope,

Many gun advocates believe that having a gun in the home can protect you from intruders.

duct tape, handcuffs, and blindfolds. Even so, some people think they should not have a gun in the home. They believe guns make society a dangerous place. Statistics support their feelings.

GUNS IN AMERICA

The United States Center for Disease Control (CDC) reports that over thirty thousand people in the United States were killed by guns in 2003.[2] Of these, 3,012 were children. This averages to one child every three hours and more than fifty children each week.[3]

The childhood death rate by guns in the United States (1.6 per 100,000 children) is nearly twelve times higher than in twenty-five other modern nations combined. The annual number of children killed by guns in Canada is around one hundred fifty. In Great Britain it is nineteen. Japan has none.[4] Each one of these countries has stricter gun control laws than the United States.

Many people in the United States would like stricter gun laws. Others would not. Those who do not say strict gun laws punish the people who use firearms responsibly. For example, thousands of people enjoy hunting and gun collecting. If guns were illegal, these people would not be able to enjoy a favored pastime.

Other people want to be able to keep guns for self-defense. Citizens of the United States have long armed themselves for protection. During the

The **National Rifle Association: Safety Programs—Eddie Eagle** handgun safety program is designed to educate young children not to handle guns. Proponents see it as a responsible effort to teach gun safety, while opponents see it as an effort to increase the attraction to guns among children. Form your viewpoint about this debate when you visit the site.

1950s, for example, some African Americans kept guns in their homes to defend themselves from attacks by hate groups such as the Ku Klux Klan.

Today, over three hundred thousand crimes are committed with firearms each year.[5] Many people believe a gun is necessary to protect themselves from becoming a victim in one of these crimes.

People also fear extraordinary circumstances that could make a gun necessary. For example, after Hurricane Katrina destroyed parts of New Orleans in 2005, there was widespread looting. Personal weapons helped some people protect their property and belongings.

Finally, people who want to keep guns legal believe the Second Amendment to the United States Constitution guarantees everyone the right to own a gun. It says, "A well regulated militia being necessary to the security of a free State, the right of the People to keep and bear arms, shall not be infringed."

Many people think this means that every United States citizen has the right to own a gun. Therefore, they say, no laws can be made that take guns from ordinary people.

THE HISTORY OF THE SECOND AMENDMENT

2

When English colonists stepped onto American soil in 1607, they carried guns. They needed them to hunt for food and to protect themselves from wild animals and some hostile American Indians.

These colonists built England's first permanent settlement in America. They named it Jamestown. The colonists also built a militia. A militia is an army of soldiers made from citizens. Militias serve their communities in emergencies.

The men in Jamestown's militia spent most of their days in pursuit of survival. The town was battered by sickness and hunger, and over half of the original colonists died. Occasionally the militia was called together for training or to protect the settlement against an American Indian attack. On these occasions, militiamen were expected to bring their own firearms.

Jamestown survived, and its success brought more European immigrants to America. Over the next century, thousands would settle on America's eastern coast. By 1750, the population of the eastern seaboard was over one million.

Most colonists kept firearms. Some used them to hunt for food. Mainly, though, colonists needed weapons for protection. The new European Americans were encroaching on American Indian land, and this sometimes led to combat between the two.

In addition, various European countries were competing for land in the New World. Each one expected its own colonists to defend territory for

the motherland. Sometimes this meant fighting.

Colonists in the South had another reason for keeping weapons. Many landowners had African slaves working the fields of their tobacco or cotton plantations. Plantation owners often used harsh treatments to keep their slaves from rebelling. Yet this did not always stop revolts. Slave owners kept firearms nearby in case of trouble.

Colonists often kept firearms in the home or carried them while they were out. In this painting called Going to Church by G. H. Boughton, these pilgrims are carrying weapons with them to religious services.

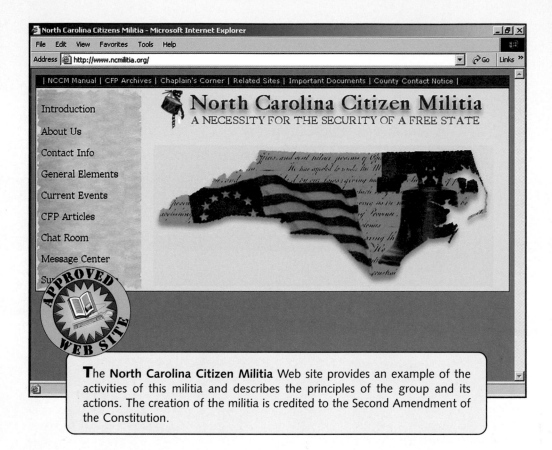

| NCCM Manual | CFP Archives | Chaplain's Corner | Related Sites | Important Documents | County Contact Notice |

Introduction

About Us

Contact Info

General Elements

Current Events

CFP Articles

Chat Room

Message Center

Su...

North Carolina Citizen Militia
A NECESSITY FOR THE SECURITY OF A FREE STATE

APPROVED WEB SITE

The **North Carolina Citizen Militia** Web site provides an example of the activities of this militia and describes the principles of the group and its actions. The creation of the militia is credited to the Second Amendment of the Constitution.

In almost every part of America, a colonist's very survival could depend on his or her skills at self-defense. Therefore, most colonists kept guns and each colony kept a militia. In fact, many colonies had laws requiring every man to keep a firearm and serve in its militia. Militia members were also required to "muster," or regularly gather for training. Failure to do so could result in a fine or punishment.

➔THE FRENCH AND INDIAN WAR

By the mid 1750s, Great Britain and France owned most of the land in America that had been settled by Europeans. But both countries wanted more. This led to a war between the two nations called the French and Indian War (1754–63). The British won, gaining control of what are now parts of Canada as well as the land between the Appalachian Mountains and the Mississippi River.

When the French and Indian War ended, British soldiers did not return to England. Instead, they roamed the streets of America. The British said their purpose was to maintain peace between the colonists and the American Indians. But some people believed they stayed for a different reason. They believed the troops stayed to help enforce the British king's new laws.

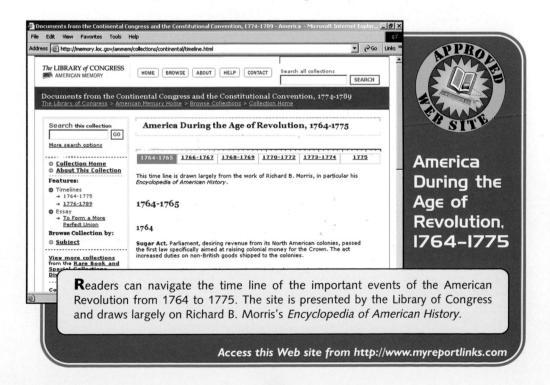

Readers can navigate the time line of the important events of the American Revolution from 1764 to 1775. The site is presented by the Library of Congress and draws largely on Richard B. Morris's *Encyclopedia of American History*.

Access this Web site from http://www.myreportlinks.com

King George III and the Parliament in Great Britain had recently begun restricting freedoms of the American colonists. Yet the colonists had been governing themselves for one hundred fifty years. They did not want a government an ocean away telling them what to do.

In addition, the British began taxing colonists more than ever before. Colonists were deeply opposed to this, too. They had no representatives in Parliament and felt that taxation without representation was unfair.

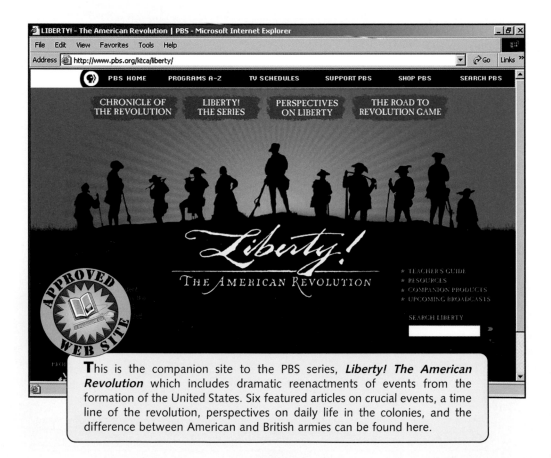

LIBERTY! – The American Revolution | PBS – Microsoft Internet Explorer

File   Edit   View   Favorites   Tools   Help

Address   http://www.pbs.org/ktca/liberty/   Go   Links

PBS HOME   PROGRAMS A–Z   TV SCHEDULES   SUPPORT PBS   SHOP PBS   SEARCH PBS

CHRONICLE OF THE REVOLUTION   LIBERTY! THE SERIES   PERSPECTIVES ON LIBERTY   THE ROAD TO REVOLUTION GAME

Liberty!

THE AMERICAN REVOLUTION

★ TEACHER'S GUIDE
★ RESOURCES
★ COMPANION PRODUCTS
★ UPCOMING BROADCASTS

SEARCH LIBERTY

This is the companion site to the PBS series, *Liberty! The American Revolution* which includes dramatic reenactments of events from the formation of the United States. Six featured articles on crucial events, a time line of the revolution, perspectives on daily life in the colonies, and the difference between American and British armies can be found here.

Then the Parliament passed the Quartering Act. This law required American colonies to feed and house the British soldiers who had stayed in America. Now Americans had to pay for soldiers they wanted to leave.

As colonists grew angrier, they grew more organized. Some formed secret clubs and pushed for others to boycott British goods. Others wrote news pamphlets explaining their views. One colonial writer penned, "quartering standing armies in a free country in times of peace without the consent of the people . . . is, and always has been deemed a violation of their rights as freemen."[1]

➲ THE QUARTERING ACT

Tensions grew and colonists in Massachusetts refused to follow the Quartering Act. This led to clashes between citizens and British soldiers. In 1770, five unarmed Boston colonists were killed when a group of British soldiers fired their guns into a protesting crowd. This became known as the Boston Massacre.

During the next few months, Revolutionary leaders talked often about the Boston Massacre. They made speeches reminding colonists of the dangers of standing armies.

Distrust of standing armies was not new. The first American colonists as well as their English ancestors had also mistrusted professionally

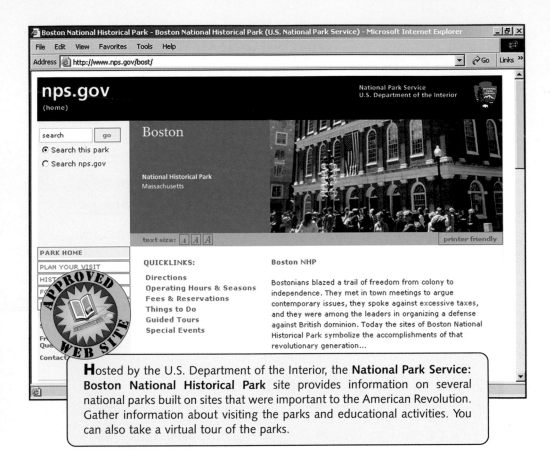

Boston National Historical Park - Boston National Historical Park (U.S. National Park Service) - Microsoft Internet Explorer

File   Edit   View   Favorites   Tools   Help

Address http://www.nps.gov/bost/   Go   Links »

nps.gov
(home)

National Park Service
U.S. Department of the Interior

search   go
◉ Search this park
◯ Search nps.gov

Boston

National Historical Park
Massachusetts

text size: A A A   printer friendly

PARK HOME

PLAN YOUR VISIT

HIST...

F...

Fr...
Que...

Contact...

QUICKLINKS:

Directions
Operating Hours & Seasons
Fees & Reservations
Things to Do
Guided Tours
Special Events

Boston NHP

Bostonians blazed a trail of freedom from colony to
independence. They met in town meetings to argue
contemporary issues, they spoke against excessive taxes,
and they were among the leaders in organizing a defense
against British dominion. Today the sites of Boston National
Historical Park symbolize the accomplishments of that
revolutionary generation...

Hosted by the U.S. Department of the Interior, the **National Park Service:
Boston National Historical Park** site provides information on several
national parks built on sites that were important to the American Revolution.
Gather information about visiting the parks and educational activities. You
can also take a virtual tour of the parks.

trained forces. This mistrust stretched back to
medieval times. Back then monarchs often used
armies to impose their will on the people. Colonial
leaders felt the British Army was just such a force.

Leaders from the colonies gathered in 1774 in
a meeting called the Continental Congress. During
the meeting, they pledged their loyalty to the
British throne. But they also asked Parliament to
repeal certain laws. One was the requirement that
colonists feed and house British soldiers.

Doubtful that Parliament would repeal the
Quartering Act, the colonial leaders told colonists to

be ready to take up arms. They warned them that they might have to fight to preserve the liberties they had come to enjoy. As a result, many colonies readied their militias.

In Massachusetts, citizens had been stockpiling arms and munitions in the town of Concord. When the British learned of this, they sent troops from Boston to take whatever supplies they could find.

But a Massachusetts group called the minutemen was ready to stop them. The minutemen were a militia unit trained to fight at "a minute's notice." Their goal was to keep the British Army from reaching Concord.

➔THE REVOLUTION BEGINS

The two groups met at Lexington, less than ten miles from Concord. They argued and someone fired a shot. This sparked a small battle and eight minutemen were killed. The British then marched on to Concord. There they were met by several hundred more militiamen. The British withdrew and headed back to Boston. All along the way, though, militiamen attacked them. By the time the king's army reached Boston, two hundred fifty British soldiers and ninety Americans had died.

Many Boston residents were terrified. They knew there would be more fighting, and they wanted to leave the city. The British offered the citizens safe passage out if they gave up their weapons.

The residents agreed and turned in their arms. But the British broke their promise and refused o let them leave. With the citizens disarmed, the British were able to take over Boston.

⮕A Standing Army

At a second Continental Congress in 1775, Congress organized an army to drive the British from Boston.

▲ *Many colonists already owned firearms when the Revolutionary War broke out. That made it easy for them to form militias and the Continental Army.*

They named George Washington its commander. The American leaders knew they needed a well-trained force to stand up to Great Britain's professional army. So Washington immediately began drilling the troops.

The Continental Army was able to drive the British from Boston. Yet the British tried to take over in several other places. By the summer of 1776, American leaders had decided they did not want to mend their relationship with Great Britain. Instead, they wanted to create an independent nation in America.

A New Nation

On July 4, 1776, the Declaration of Independence announced the formation of the United States. Each of the American colonies would become an independent state. These states would soon join together to form one country. Not long after declaring independence, colonial leaders began writing state constitutions.

The constitutions listed the rights of the people who lived in a particular state. Most said citizens had the right to free speech and to practice the religion of their choosing. Many declared the right to a free press. Several stressed a dislike for standing armies and a belief that the best way to defend a state was with an effective militia.

Colonists felt that the right to form militias was vital to the existence of the colony. How else could

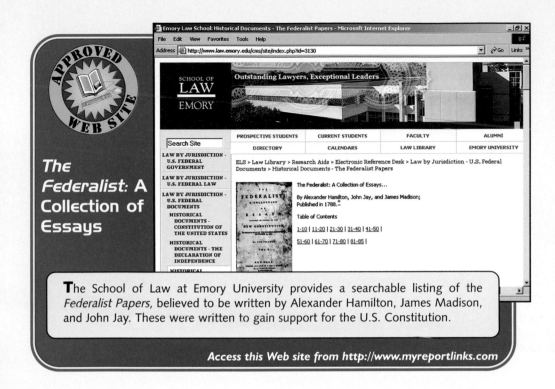

The School of Law at Emory University provides a searchable listing of the *Federalist Papers*, believed to be written by Alexander Hamilton, James Madison, and John Jay. These were written to gain support for the U.S. Constitution.

Access this Web site from http://www.myreportlinks.com

they protect their freedoms against standing armies? But Revolutionary leaders knew that militias alone would not be able to push the British from America. So they never disbanded the Continental Army.

This had the effect of creating two fighting forces—a central army and the militia. Militias were not usually successful when battling the British alone. However, they were valuable when fighting alongside the Continental Army. So as often as possible, military leaders used both.

Great Britain won many of the early battles against the colonists. Yet the Americans refused to give up.

In 1777, France began to support the revolutionaries. It provided them with money and military equipment. This tipped the scales in America's favor, and the colonists began winning battles.

In October 1781 the British finally surrendered. It would take another two years to work out the terms of peace. The war officially ended in 1783 with the signing of the Treaty of Paris. The United States of America was now a real nation.

FEDERALISTS AND ANTI-FEDERALISTS

While some American leaders were busy negotiating the peace treaty, others were creating a new government. The states would be organized into a country by the guidelines in a document called the Articles of Confederation. It soon became clear that the Articles of Confederation would not work.

In 1787, United States leaders gathered together again. They wanted to write a different contract for the nation. It would be called the Constitution. The Constitution would outline the basic principles by which the United States would operate.

Writing the Constitution was not easy. Various people had many ideas about how to create one nation from thirteen separate states. Two opposing points of view would emerge.

One view was held by a group known as the Federalists. The Federalists wanted the nation to have a powerful central government. They

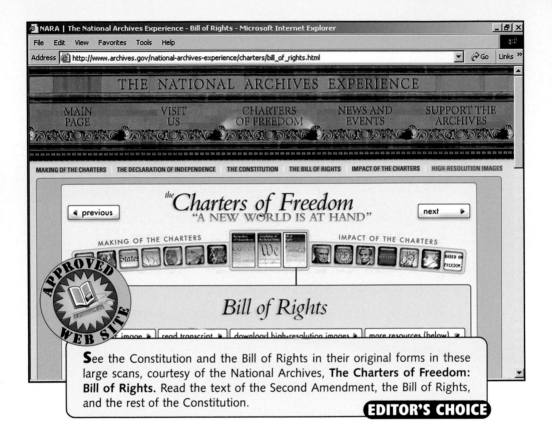

See the Constitution and the Bill of Rights in their original forms in these large scans, courtesy of the National Archives, **The Charters of Freedom: Bill of Rights**. Read the text of the Second Amendment, the Bill of Rights, and the rest of the Constitution.

EDITOR'S CHOICE

believed this would make the new country strong and secure.

The other group, though, feared placing too much power in one body. People who felt this way were called the Anti-Federalists. Anti-Federalists wanted the state governments to remain strong and for the central government to not have a lot of power over the states. These state governments would be independent of other states and any central government.

These two points of view led to differences of opinion about many topics. For example, Federalists believed the country needed one strong army to protect its citizens. They believed that all of the state militias should be put under federal control.

Anti-Federalists, however, did not want a central army. How, they asked, would this be different from Great Britain's professional army the Americans had just defeated? They felt that any constitution must protect the people from a ruler's unjust use of a standing army.

⇒THE BILL OF RIGHTS

After months of work and discussion, the United States Constitution was ready to be sent to the states. In order for it to become law, nine states had to approve, or ratify, the document.

Not all of the state legislatures were happy with the Constitution. They wanted the federal government to guarantee it would not intrude on certain freedoms. Some states insisted that the Constitution include a declaration of citizens' liberties.

So the leaders went back to work writing an addition to the Constitution. It would list rights that the federal government could not take away from the citizens or the states. Each right would be specifically spelled out in a separate amendment. The addition would be called the Bill of Rights. James Madison was called upon to write the document.

→WRITING THE SECOND AMENDMENT

Madison knew the Bill of Rights must address the concerns of the state leaders. Many had worried about placing too much military power in the hands of a central government. They feared the federal government would either do away with state militias or take away rights that gave militias power. Several states wanted the new document to mention the people's right to bear arms. New Hampshire wanted an amendment that said Congress could not disarm a citizen.[2]

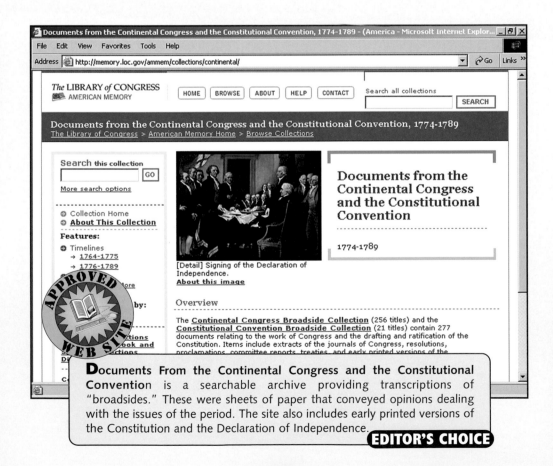

Documents From the Continental Congress and the Constitutional Convention is a searchable archive providing transcriptions of "broadsides." These were sheets of paper that conveyed opinions dealing with the issues of the period. The site also includes early printed versions of the Constitution and the Declaration of Independence.

EDITOR'S CHOICE

In addition to reviewing these suggestions, Madison looked at various state constitutions for ideas. Most emphasized the role of militias in the defense of a state. A few included the right to bear arms. One included the right to keep arms.

Finally, Madison was ready to write the Second Amendment. His words closely followed Virginia's state constitution. It said "That a well-regulated Militia, composed of the body of the people, trained to arms, is the proper, natural and safe defense of a free State; that Standing Armies, in time of peace, should be avoided as dangerous to liberty . . ."[3]

Madison's version read, "A well-regulated militia, composed of the body of the people, being the best security of a free country, the right of the people to keep and bear arms shall not be infringed . . . [and] . . . no person religiously scrupulous shall be compelled to bear arms."[4]

Madison had added the phrase about religious exemptions out of respect for people of certain faiths. Some, like the Quakers, were pacifists. A pacifist is a person who lives by the deep conviction that violence is unacceptable.

⮕DISCUSSING THE SECOND AMENDMENT

Once finished, the Bill of Rights was submitted to the House of Representatives. Members discussed the amendment. Some did not like the phrase that exempted pacifists from duty. They thought it might be misused by people who simply did not want to serve in a militia. The words were deleted.

Next the amendment went to the Senate. It made changes of its own, mostly condensing the wording. It also changed the words "free country" to "free state."

During all of the debate over the wording of the Second Amendment, legislators spent much time talking about the role the military would play in the federal government. The lawmakers focused mainly on the Federalist versus Anti-Federalist philosophies. One central concern was assuring states they would have the right to keep militias. Congressional records from the time do not mention any discussions regarding a citizen's right to bear arms for non-militia purposes.[5]

Once all parties were satisfied, Congress ratified the version we know today. It read, "A well regulated militia being necessary to the security of a free State, the right of the People to keep and bear arms, shall not be infringed."

With the Bill of Rights attached, the Constitution was sent back to the states. They approved it, and it became the law of the land in 1791.

INDIVIDUAL OR COLLECTIVE RIGHT?

T he meaning of the Second Amendment has been the subject of much debate. Everyone is in agreement that the amendment guarantees United States citizens the right to bear arms. However, people disagree about what bearing arms actually means.

⊖AN INDIVIDUAL RIGHT

Do the words "bear arms" mean that every person has an undeniable right to own a gun? Some people say yes. This point of view has become known as the individual rights view. Supporters of individual rights believe gun owner-ship is a right as fundamental and basic as the freedom of speech. These people believe that owning a gun repre-sents a person's ability to defend his or her life. This, they say, is a natural right and belongs to every human being.

Individual rights proponents say that bearing arms is also about the ability of a population to protect its free-dom. Unarmed populations, they say, are helpless against governments who wish to take away liberties. These gov-ernments often have well-armed, well-trained armies that follow any orders they are given. If a tyrannical ruler directs an army to take away people's rights, an unarmed population is not able to defend its freedom. Believers in individual rights think that an armed citizenry is necessary to protect personal liberties.[1]

A perfect example, they say, is the American Revolution. The British seizure of arms in Boston shows how an ironhanded government must take away the people's weapons in order to rule. Being armed and ready to fight was vital to the Americans at the beginning of the war. Without groups like the minutemen, the American Revolution might never have happened.

Individual rights proponents believe the revolutionary experience was fresh in the minds of the writers of the Second Amendment. These leaders knew it was vital for individual citizens to be armed should they ever need to revolt. Because of this, they say, those who wrote the Second Amendment were protecting an individual's right to bear arms.

A COLLECTIVE RIGHT

Other people disagree with this interpretation. They believe the first phrase of the amendment is the key to understanding its meaning. They say, "A well regulated militia being necessary to the security of a free state," is referring to the people's right to form militias.

People with this view believe that the writers of the Second Amendment were not speaking of an individual's right to bear arms. They believe the writers were referring to a state's right to form militias. This is called the collective rights theory.

People who believe in collective rights point to the Anti-Federalists and their fear of standing armies. Anti-Federalists believed that the best protection against a professional army was a militia. Militias were made of ordinary citizens from local communities. They were groups authorized by a state government to possess weapons. These people had ties to, and interests in, the lives of the people around them. A force such as this would be reluctant to take away the rights and freedoms of their neighbors.

▲ This is a reenactment of colonial militiamen fighting the Battle of Fort Henry during the Revolutionary War. The colonial militia played a large role in the Revolutionary War.

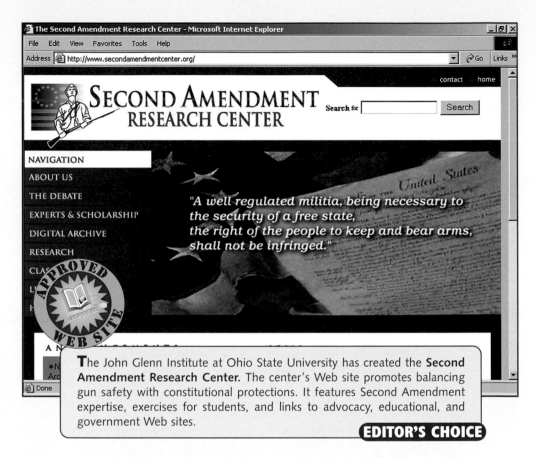

The Second Amendment Research Center - Microsoft Internet Explorer

File   Edit   View   Favorites   Tools   Help

Address http://www.secondamendmentcenter.org/   Go   Links »

contact   home

SECOND AMENDMENT
RESEARCH CENTER   Search for [   ]   [Search]

NAVIGATION

ABOUT US

THE DEBATE

EXPERTS & SCHOLARSHIP

DIGITAL ARCHIVE

RESEARCH

"A well-regulated militia, being necessary to the security of a free state, the right of the people to keep and bear arms, shall not be infringed."

The John Glenn Institute at Ohio State University has created the **Second Amendment Research Center.** The center's Web site promotes balancing gun safety with constitutional protections. It features Second Amendment expertise, exercises for students, and links to advocacy, educational, and government Web sites.

EDITOR'S CHOICE

Furthermore, in the days of the Constitution's writing, militia members were expected to use their own weapons. Therefore, the amendment was saying people could own arms for fighting in a militia.

Proponents of the collective rights theory point out that although the colonists created the Continental Army to fight the British, this army was disbanded soon after the war ceased being waged. No professional army was created in its place. American leaders must have believed, then, that the new nation wanted state militias to handle the people's defense needs.

Collective rights proponents also look at the Militia Act of 1792. This law was passed just after the Constitution and the Bill of Rights were ratified. It called for all able-bodied white men between the ages of eighteen and forty-five to serve in a militia. It required that every militiaman report to duty with a "good musket or firelock." The Second Amendment, they say, was written to protect a state's right to maintain just such a militia.

THE BRANCHES OF THE GOVERNMENT

Over the years, people who believe the Second Amendment protects an individual's right to bear arms have had deep disagreements with people who think the amendment is about a collective right. The writers of the Constitution foresaw conflicts of opinion about how rights might be interpreted. So they set up a system to peacefully work out these disagreements. This system divides the United States government into three parts called branches: the legislative branch, the executive branch, and the judicial branch.

Each branch of the government has a job. Congress makes up the legislative branch. Its job is to make laws. The most important person in the executive branch is the president. The president enforces the law. The third branch of the government is called the judicial branch. Its job is to make sure that laws follow the Constitution. While national,

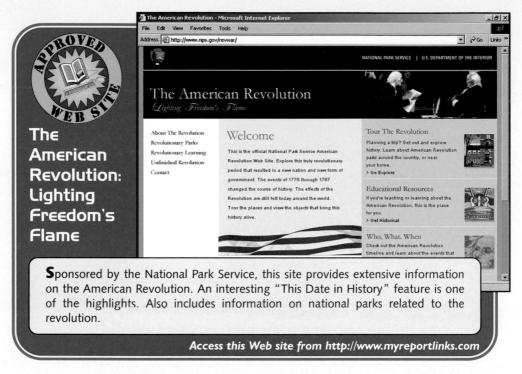

Sponsored by the National Park Service, this site provides extensive information on the American Revolution. An interesting "This Date in History" feature is one of the highlights. Also includes information on national parks related to the revolution.

Access this Web site from http://www.myreportlinks.com

state, and local governments can make their own laws, none of these laws can interfere with the ideas set forth in the Constitution.

To help the judicial branch oversee laws, the nation's founders created a court called the Supreme Court. The Supreme Court is called upon when there is a question about the constitutionality of a law.

→THE SUPREME COURT

The Supreme Court is made up of nine people called justices. The president of the United States appoints each justice to the Court. The Senate must then approve of this person. Once appointed, a Supreme Court justice can stay on the Court for his or her entire life.

Before a case can be brought before the Supreme Court it must have been heard in a "lower" court—a state court, or federal district court. If a person thinks that this court has made a mistake, that person can appeal the case. This means asking a higher-level court to review the case. But an appeal cannot be made to the Supreme Court simply because a person does not like a ruling. It can only be made if someone has a good reason to believe that a court has not followed proper procedure or has ruled in a way that goes against the state or United States Constitution.

A case may go through several courts as people appeal rulings. The final court to hear an appeal is the Supreme Court. It is the highest court in the United States and its ruling is final.

⊜Only a Handful of Cases

Yet the Supreme Court does not hear all of the cases it is asked to consider. In fact, it hears very few. Each year, the justices choose a handful of cases to judge from the thousands it is asked to review. These cases are often the ones justices think will help clarify the meaning of the Constitution.

Before deciding on a case, the justices listen to presentations from lawyers on each side of the issue. These presentations are called arguments. During an argument, justices ask questions about the

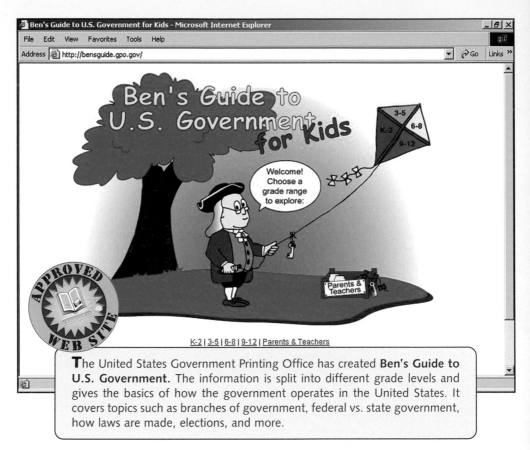

K-2 | 3-5 | 6-8 | 9-12 | Parents & Teachers

The United States Government Printing Office has created **Ben's Guide to U.S. Government.** The information is split into different grade levels and gives the basics of how the government operates in the United States. It covers topics such as branches of government, federal vs. state government, how laws are made, elections, and more.

case and the Constitution. Then the justices meet privately to talk more about the case. Finally, they vote.

→ SUPREME COURT OPINIONS

Cases are decided by majority vote. A justice who has voted with the majority writes a report about the ruling on the case. This is called the opinion of the court. Of course, not all of the justices may agree with this vote. Those who disagree form a group called the dissenting opinion. A justice from this group also writes a report. It tells why he or she disagrees with the majority's opinion.

Another kind of report may be written. It is called a concurring opinion. A concurring opinion is written by a justice from the majority side that agrees with a ruling, but has a different reason for doing so. All of the opinions issued by the Supreme Court are published in an official record.

➔ STARE DECISIS

In general, the Supreme Court interprets the Constitution the same way prior courts have. This is called *stare decisis*. *Stare decisis* means that when a case comes before the Court, the justices look back at previous rulings in cases with similar questions. The Court usually follows the reasoning of past decisions.

Occasionally, though, the Supreme Court sees a past decision as wrong. If so, it may rule in an

▲ *The Supreme Court in 2007. Seated left to right are Anthony M. Kennedy, John Paul Stevens, Chief Justice John G. Roberts, Jr., Antonin Scalia, and David H. Souter. Standing left to right are Stephen G. Breyer, Clarence Thomas, Ruth Bader Ginsburg, and Samuel Alito, Jr.*

opposite manner. It might also rule in the opposite manner when it decides a lower court is wrong. Changing a previous ruling is called overturning or reversing a decision.

The Court might change a ruling because there are changes in society. For example, in 1896, the Supreme Court ruled in *Plessy* v. *Ferguson* that it was acceptable to have "separate but equal" facilities for white people and black people. But by the mid-1950s this kind of segregation was seen as discriminatory. In a 1954 case called *Brown* v. *Board of Education,* the Supreme Court overturned *Plessy* v. *Ferguson* by ruling that racially separated schools were unequal and unconstitutional.

Sometimes the Court changes rulings because the justices who make up the Court change. Different justices have different opinions about the meaning of the Constitution. When a group of like-minded justices serve on the Court at the same time, their decisions create a pattern of interpretation. If justices with different opinions begin forming the Court, the pattern of decisions might change.

THE BILL OF RIGHTS AND THE SUPREME COURT

The Supreme Court has heard hundreds of cases. Most question how much power the government should have controlling citizens' behaviors. Some Constitutional amendments have been tested

Discover a great variety of information at the online resource for the **Supreme Court of the United States.** This site describes the building and how the court operates, provides biographies of the Justices, and gives information about Supreme Court decisions.

more than others. Ideas in the First Amendment, for example, have been examined many times. But in comparison, the Court has heard very few cases about the Second Amendment.[2]

Each time the Court gives its ruling on a Second Amendment case, people study its decision carefully. They read the opinions closely, trying to decide whether the Court believes the Second Amendment refers to an individual or collective right to bear arms. The Court's rulings have not always provided a clear answer.[3]

4 THE SECOND AMENDMENT IN COURT: 1785–1960

*I*n the country's early years, there was little public debate about the meaning of the Second Amendment. The country was growing westward, and life was full of dangers. It would have been impractical for a nation that wanted to grow to limit people's personal ownership of weapons.

In addition, the nation's leadership still valued militias. Henry Knox, the United States secretary of war from 1785–1794, believed that service in a militia should be a requirement for any rights as a free citizen. He proposed a system of camps around the country where local men would receive militia training.

Many presidents supported this view. President Thomas Jefferson once told Congress, "[F]or a people who are free, and who mean to remain so, a well organized militia is their best security."[1] This deep belief in the value of and need for a working militia led to the Militia Act of 1792.

The new nation did in fact depend on the state militias in the country's early years. The Continental

Army had been disbanded after the Revolutionary War, and the United States maintained only a small fighting force. Therefore, state militias handled almost all security problems themselves. This most often meant battling American Indians.

➔THE WAR OF 1812

State militias were not always effective forces. For instance, they were of small value during the War of 1812. This war between the United States and Great Britain was fought mainly for two reasons. First, some United States officials wanted to take land from the British in what is now Canada. Second, the United

▲ *Of the founding fathers, Thomas Jefferson was one of the biggest supporters of requiring citizens to serve in a state militia. Jefferson is in the center of this illustration, a portion of a painting called* Signing of the Declaration of Independence, *by John Trumbull.*

States wanted the British Navy to stop boarding American ships at sea to search for British deserters.

The United States declared war on Great Britain in 1812. President James Madison called on state militias to help fight. But several states refused to send troops. Others sent only a fraction of what had been requested. Many men who did show up for duty refused to serve beyond their required six-month term.

With troop levels low, the British were able to land off the coast of Maryland and march to Washington, D.C. Once there, the British burned the Capitol building and the White House.

Alarmed, many Americans enlisted in the national army. This enabled United States military forces to drive the British from America. When the war ended in 1814, the state militias were sent home and Congress again reduced the number of troops in the federal army.

At the time, many people warned that state militias could not adequately defend the country. But most leaders of the time were more interested in westward expansion than in national defense.

GUNS IN A GROWING NATION

Yet guns remained a vital part of everyday life. Owning a gun for service in a militia was still common. More common, though, was gun ownership for personal needs—protection on the frontier, defense against slave rebellions, and the occasional hunt for meat.

As new states joined the nation they wrote their own constitutions. Many left out any mention of bearing arms for the common defense of the state or the nation. Instead, state constitutions emphasized an individual's right to bear arms.

For nearly half a century there were no court cases in the United States related to the Second Amendment. When one finally did come up, it never went past the state level.

▲ During the War of 1812 some states were slow to send troops to defend Washington, D.C. As a result, the troops there were overrun and the White House and Capitol building were burned. This painting is an illustrator's depiction of how the scene may have looked.

➔ *BLISS V. KENTUCKY*

In 1822, a Kentucky man named Bliss was arrested for carrying a sword hidden in a cane. This violated a Kentucky law that said people could not carry concealed weapons.

Bliss was found guilty and fined one hundred dollars. But he believed the law violated his state's constitution. One section of it said "the right of the citizens to bear arms in [defense] of themselves and the state, shall not be questioned."[2] Bliss appealed his conviction to the Kentucky Court of Appeals.

The Kentucky Court of Appeals agreed with Bliss. It said that according to Kentucky's constitution, laws could not be made that interfered with an individual's right to bear arms. This right was not restricted to weapons easily seen. Whether concealed or not, ruled the court, Bliss had a right to carry a sword.

Therefore, the court decided that the law Bliss was arrested under violated the state's constitution. This ruling gave legal standing to an individual interpretation of the right to bear arms.

Still, *Bliss v. Kentucky* (1822) was not a true test of the Second Amendment. It would not be until 1833 that the country's highest court would hear a case affecting the Second Amendment. Ironically, this case was not even about guns.

➡ *Barron v. Baltimore*

Barron v. *Baltimore* (1833) was brought before the Court by John Barron. Barron owned a dock in Baltimore and unloaded ships for a living. As part of a program to improve the streets, Baltimore

▲ *A man conceals a gun in his belt and waistband. Whether someone has the right to carry concealed weapons has been challenged since 1822.*

changed the flow of several streams throughout the city. Their new paths took sand and gravel into the water around Barron's wharf. Soon the water there was too shallow for large ships to dock, and they had to unload elsewhere. This caused Barron to lose business.

Barron sued the city. His lawyer argued that Baltimore was depriving him of his right to private property as stated in the Fifth Amendment of the Bill of Rights. The Fifth Amendment says that private property cannot be taken for public use without the government paying for it. Barron's attorney said that this amendment applied to states as well as to the federal government. Baltimore's actions, therefore, were unconstitutional.

THE COURT SIDES WITH BALTIMORE

After a series of lower court decisions and appeals, Barron took his case to the United States Supreme Court. The Supreme Court unanimously disagreed with Barron. The Court said that the Bill of Rights applied only to federal law. It said, "The Constitution was ordained and established by the people of the United States for themselves, for their own government, and not for the government of the individual States."[3]

Each state, it went on to say, had its own constitution that set limits on laws. Therefore, people who felt their rights were violated by a state or

EDITED BY PHILIP B. KURLAND AND RALPH LERNER

Contents

About Founders

Help

THE FOUNDERS' CONSTITUTION

This Web Edition is a joint venture of the University of Chicago Press and the Liberty Fund.

Contents | About Founders | Help

The Founders' Constitution

This is a searchable online version of a book compiled by two professors for the University of Chicago Press. The site presents a collection of writings about constitutional issues from the 1600s to the 1800s. Also included are documents, court cases, and opinions.

Access this Web site from http://www.myreportlinks.com

local government could only take action against them in a state or local court.[4]

Although this ruling said nothing about guns, the Court was setting a principle to be applied to all of the rights listed in the Constitution. The Supreme Court had decided that state laws and actions were not bound by the Bill of Rights. Under the reasoning of *Barron* v. *Baltimore,* then, the Second Amendment pertained only to federal laws about guns. States had the right to make their own gun laws. This reasoning would have an impact on gun laws for years to come.

By the middle of the nineteenth century, owning a gun in order to serve in a state militia was not the responsibility it had once been. Many state militias trained either sporadically or not at all.

Some people saw this as a danger to a free nation. As early as 1833, Supreme Court Justice Joseph Story had forewarned that, ". . . among the American people there is a growing indifference to any system of militia discipline . . . There is certainly no small danger, that indifference may . . . gradually undermine all the protection intended by this clause of our national bill of rights."[5] Even so, bearing arms increasingly meant having a weapon for personal use.

➔ NUNN V. GEORGIA

Georgia's Supreme Court illustrated this in the case of Nunn v. Georgia in 1846. In this case, Hawkins H. Nunn had been convicted of carrying a concealed weapon. Georgia law prohibited this, but Hawkins believed the law violated his Second Amendment rights. He took his case to the Georgia Supreme Court.

Unlike Kentucky, Georgia's supreme court said the state could make a law prohibiting people from carrying concealed weapons. Yet the court told Georgia lawmakers they could not completely take away a citizen's right to bear arms.[6] They said this right was protected. Georgia, like Kentucky, believed in an individual right to own a firearm.

⊖The Civil War

By the time the Civil War broke out in 1861, state militias were in complete disarray. People on both sides of the conflict refused to answer their state's call to duty. Those who did were only required to serve for three months. Many left when their time was over—even if this was in the middle of a battle.

This forced the North and the South to call for volunteers. More soldiers were still needed, though, so Congress passed a law requiring men in the North to enlist in its army.

By the end of the fighting in 1865, more than six hundred thousand soldiers had died. But the war

▲ By the 1830s it was no longer necessary to join a state militia. Most gun owners bought them for hunting or other personal uses.

had kept the nation together and freed 4 million slaves.

Yet some Southerners did not want to give former slaves equal rights. They made laws limiting their freedoms. These laws became known as Black Codes. Black Codes treated former slaves as second-class citizens, restricting their rights and liberties. For example, African Americans in some states were not allowed to own firearms.

⊖THE FOURTEENTH AMENDMENT

The nation's lawmakers believed that Black Codes were a violation of the rights of African Americans. They wrote an amendment to the Constitution to make them illegal. The Fourteenth Amendment granted full citizenship rights to former slaves. It said that all states must provide equal protection under the law to all persons. The Fourteenth Amendment was ratified in 1868.

Now new questions arose. The Fourteenth Amendment said that no state could "deprive any person of life, liberty, or property without due process of law; nor deny to any person within its jurisdiction the equal protection of the laws." The amendment seemed to indicate that there were certain rights states had to extend to its citizens. Those rights were the ones related to life, liberty, or property. In legal terms, these rights were now "incorporated" against the states.

Many scholars wondered exactly which rights these were. Did they include all of the rights in the Bill of Rights? If they only included some, was the Second Amendment one? If so, did this mean the amendment was about an individual's right to bear arms?

The Fourteenth Amendment angered some whites. They did not want to extend equal rights to

▲ These men are taking part in a Civil War reenactment. When the Civil War broke out, many state militias were in disarray. As a result, the Union had to pass a law forcing people to enlist in the Army.

black people. Some whites rebelled by harassing blacks whenever they could. This sometimes had violent consequences. One encounter turned deadly in 1872.

That year the people of Louisiana elected a governor whom many white people did not like. In a direct act of rebellion, some whites formed a militant group called the White League. The White League attacked black people all over the state.

An assault that took place in the town of Colfax was particularly violent. There, a mob of White League members was met by an all-black unit of the state militia. The White League shot into the militia, killing one hundred blacks. Three whites also died. This incident became known as the Colfax Massacre.

➔ *U.S. v. CRUIKSHANK*

The United States government arrested the leaders of the massacre. The whites were convicted of interfering with the constitutional rights of the black militiamen.

The men appealed their conviction to the Supreme Court. Their case, *U.S. v. Cruikshank* (1876), would be the first Supreme Court case directly related to the Second Amendment. One of the questions before the Court was whether the men had deprived the victims of their Second Amendment rights.

The Supreme Court ruled for the defendants. It stated that it did not have the power to rule on one citizen's actions against another citizen. The Court was not approving of what the white men had done. It was saying the federal courts did not have the authority to judge them.

In its majority opinion, the Court said that the Fourteenth Amendment added nothing to the rights of "one citizen as against another. It simply furnishes an additional guaranty against any encroachment by the States upon the fundamental rights which belong to every citizen . . ."[7] In other words, the Fourteenth Amendment only protected citizens from government actions that took away liberties.

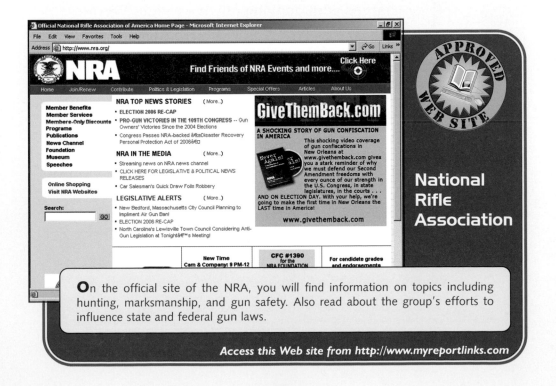

On the official site of the NRA, you will find information on topics including hunting, marksmanship, and gun safety. Also read about the group's efforts to influence state and federal gun laws.

Access this Web site from http://www.myreportlinks.com

▲ In 1876, the Supreme Court heard U.S. v. Cruikshank, the first case to directly challenge a group's Second Amendment rights.

In *U.S.* v. *Cruikshank,* there was no government being charged with denying anyone rights. Therefore, there was no issue the Supreme Court could address. Any action to correct wrongs committed by one person against another would have to be taken to a state court.

PRESSER V. ILLINOIS

Ten years later, the Supreme Court heard another case related to the Second Amendment. In *Presser* v. *Illinois* (1886), Herman Presser led a parade of rifle-bearing men through Chicago, Illinois. The men were members of a German Nationalist organization.

But Illinois law prohibited any group other than the regular organized state militia to drill or parade with arms. Presser was convicted of violating the law. He appealed his conviction, claiming the law deprived him of his Second Amendment rights.

The Supreme Court did not agree. It upheld the Illinois law, saying the states have the authority to control and regulate military bodies. This, it said, included the drilling and parading of military groups.

The Court noted that the Illinois law did not ban an individual from having a firearm. It said this would be unconstitutional since it would interfere with the government's ability to raise a militia from the general population.

THE DICK ACT

By the end of the nineteenth century, though, most state militias had nearly collapsed. In 1901, President Theodore Roosevelt called the militia system "obsolete and worthless."[8] At the time, the nation's central standing army was less than thirty thousand men strong. President Roosevelt warned Congress that the United States lacked any kind of effective defense.

Soon after, Congress passed laws called the Dick Act. The purpose of the Dick Act was to strengthen the state militias. Militias would now receive money from the federal government. In addition, they would be trained by officers in the regular army.

A few years later, President Woodrow Wilson wanted to expand the use of the militias. He asked

Congress for a law that said militias could be used in foreign countries. In response, Congress passed the National Defense Act of 1916.

When the United States entered World War I in 1917, many militia units were drafted and sent overseas. A few cases challenged the federal government's authority to use militias this way. But courts upheld Congress's right to call the units to duty.

A NEW MILITIA—THE NATIONAL GUARD

In 1933, a law officially changed the name of all state militias to the National Guard. The law also made the National Guard units part of the United States Army.

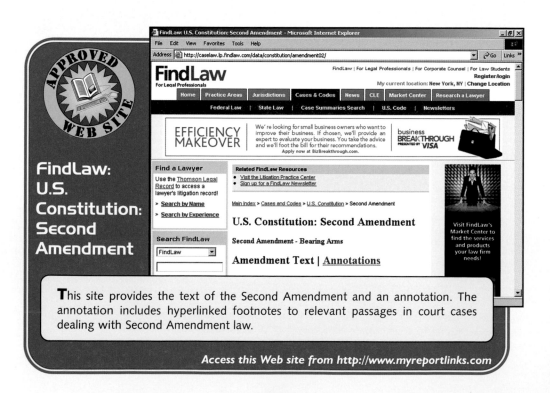

FindLaw: U.S. Constitution: Second Amendment

This site provides the text of the Second Amendment and an annotation. The annotation includes hyperlinked footnotes to relevant passages in court cases dealing with Second Amendment law.

Access this Web site from http://www.myreportlinks.com

These forces would still be available to individual states. Congress had given control of the units to both the state and federal governments. Either one could call them to action.

But now the United States Army would provide the National Guards with training, uniforms, and a salary. It would also provide them with all of the weapons and ammunition they needed for duty. And now the National Guards were an official part of a federal military force—the United States Army.

⇒THE NATIONAL FIREARMS ACT

During the 1920s and 1930s, American society faced growing violence. Much of it was a result of Prohibition, a law that prohibited the sale of alcoholic beverages.

Many Americans thought Prohibition infringed on their personal freedom. So they bought liquor illegally from people called bootleggers. Bootleggers often belonged to gangs organized for the purpose of selling alcohol.

Rivalries developed between gangsters as they competed for business and territory. These rivalries led to gang wars that sometimes ended in murder. The most popular weapons used by these criminals were machine guns.

Well aware of Second Amendment issues, lawmakers were also concerned about violence on

America's streets. Many felt it was their duty to make the nation safer. So Congress decided it would regulate the guns gangsters used. It could do so using the authority it was given under the Commerce Clause of the Constitution.

The Commerce Clause says that Congress can "regulate commerce with foreign nations, among the several States, and with the Indian Tribes." With this idea in mind, Congress wrote a new law.

The National Firearms Act of 1934 said that automatic weapons and sawed-off shotguns had to be taxed and registered with the federal government. This, thought Congress, met the constitutional demands of the Second Amendment.

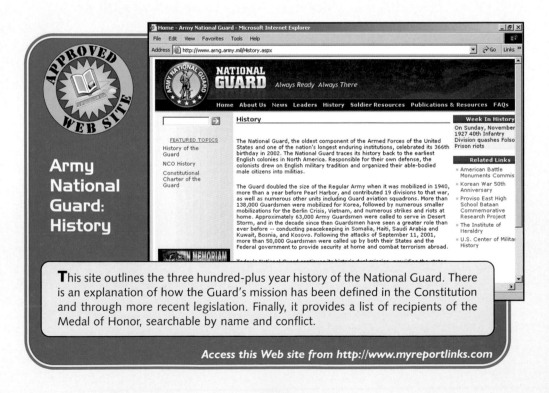

Army National Guard: History

This site outlines the three hundred-plus year history of the National Guard. There is an explanation of how the Guard's mission has been defined in the Constitution and through more recent legislation. Finally, it provides a list of recipients of the Medal of Honor, searchable by name and conflict.

Access this Web site from http://www.myreportlinks.com

At the same time it would stop people from using certain weapons for illegal purposes.

However, some people did not think the National Firearms Act was constitutional. They believed Congress was overstepping its authority. They believed the new laws were more about gun regulation than commerce regulation. They felt that the National Firearms Act violated the Second Amendment.

⊜MILLER AND LAYTON

The first people to test the law's constitutionality were Jack Miller and Frank Layton. In 1937, police who suspected they were involved in a bank robbery stopped them. They found an unregistered sawed-off shotgun in the men's vehicle. Miller and Layton admitted they had taken the weapon from Oklahoma to Arkansas. As a result, they were found guilty of violating the National Firearms Act.

However, both men thought that the National Firearms Act infringed on their Second Amendment rights. They felt the Constitution gave them the right to carry any weapon they wanted without restriction. So they appealed their conviction to a higher court.

This court agreed with Miller and Layton. The United States government then asked the Supreme Court to review the case. Its decision in the case is the most thorough and specific ruling the Court

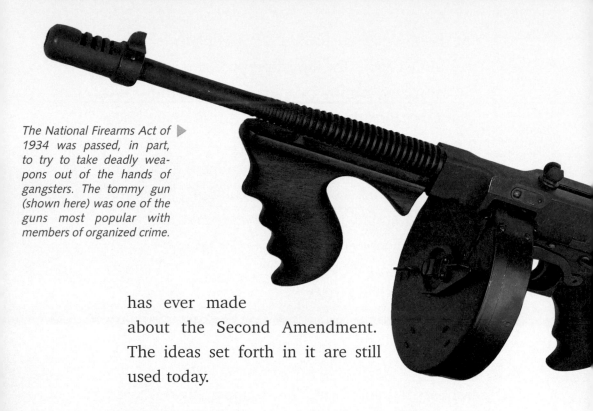

The National Firearms Act of 1934 was passed, in part, to try to take deadly weapons out of the hands of gangsters. The tommy gun (shown here) was one of the guns most popular with members of organized crime.

has ever made about the Second Amendment. The ideas set forth in it are still used today.

U.S. V. MILLER

In *U.S. v. Miller* (1939), the Supreme Court unanimously disagreed with Miller and Layton. The Court ruled that the National Firearms Act was constitutional.

The opinion of the Court explained the justices' reasoning. The Supreme Court had analyzed the case by looking back at the original purpose of the Second Amendment. The amendment, the Court said, was written to guarantee states the right to form their own military units.[9] The nation's founders wanted to assure states that they would be able to protect themselves from the army of an unjust federal government.

The justices decided that Miller and Layton's sawed-off shotgun had nothing to do with this right. They were not in a militia, nor was their weapon the kind used by the military. Consequently, the Court said, the Second Amendment did not apply to them. The National Firearms Act did. The conviction stood, with the Court noting that their historical analysis of the Second Amendment was how the right to bear arms should be judged.[10]

According to *U.S.* v. *Miller,* the Second Amendment does not protect a person's right to own a gun for personal use. It does not give people the right to keep weapons for self-defense, sport shooting, gun collecting, or any use other than militia service.[11] The right to bear arms as stated in the Second Amendment is only for the "preservation or efficiency of a well regulated militia."[12]

This ruling seems to directly contradict the individual rights theory of the right to bear arms. Indeed, many experts view *U.S.* v. *Miller* as a collective rights interpretation of the Second Amendment.[13]

Finally, the opinion in *U.S.* v. *Miller* discussed and defined the word "militia" as it is used in the

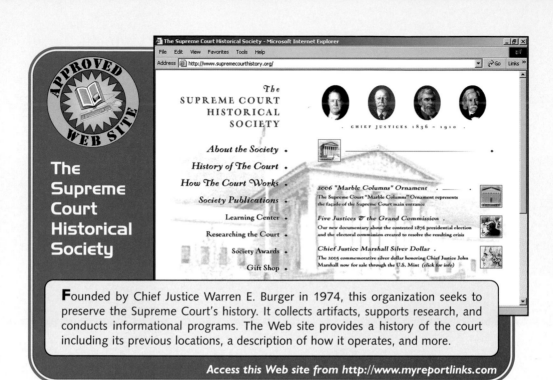

The Supreme Court Historical Society

The Supreme Court Historical Society - Microsoft Internet Explorer

File   Edit   View   Favorites   Tools   Help

Address http://www.supremecourthistory.org/   Go   Links

The SUPREME COURT HISTORICAL SOCIETY

CHIEF JUSTICES 1836 ~ 1910

About the Society

History of The Court

How The Court Works

Society Publications

Learning Center

Researching the Court

Society Awards

Gift Shop

2006 "Marble Columns" Ornament
The Supreme Court "Marble Columns" Ornament represents the façade of the Supreme Court main entrance

Five Justices & the Grand Commission
Our new documentary about the contested 1876 presidential election and the electoral commission created to resolve the resulting crisis

Chief Justice Marshall Silver Dollar
The 2005 commemorative silver dollar honoring Chief Justice John Marshall now for sale through the U.S. Mint (click for info)

Founded by Chief Justice Warren E. Burger in 1974, this organization seeks to preserve the Supreme Court's history. It collects artifacts, supports research, and conducts informational programs. The Web site provides a history of the court including its previous locations, a description of how it operates, and more.

Access this Web site from http://www.myreportlinks.com

Second Amendment. The meaning of the word had long been the subject of debate.

American colonists used the word militia to refer to an army of citizens. To them, a militia was a group of ordinary, everyday individuals. During colonial times, in fact, all able-bodied men had to belong to a militia. Therefore, to some people, the Constitution used the word militia as another word for people.[14] This would mean, then, that the Second Amendment states that every person has the right to own a gun.

However, in *U.S.* v. *Miller,* the Supreme Court did not agree with this definition. The Court said that a militia was "a body of citizens enrolled for military discipline."[15] It went on to say that a militia was a government approved and directed group. According to the 1939 opinion, militias were groups with government endorsement.[16]

➔A SECOND AMENDMENT PRECEDENT

The Supreme Court's ruling in *U.S.* v. *Miller* has set a standard for other courts to use when deciding what kinds of gun laws governments can and cannot make. A ruling that sets a standard is called a precedent. A precedent is used as an example for future decisions.

▲ *Many Americans, both men and women, "bear arms."*

As *U.S.* v. *Miller* was making its way through the courts, Congress was writing another gun law. This one was called the Federal Firearms Act of 1938. It required anyone who sold guns from one state to another to have a Federal Firearms License.

In addition, the new law required gun dealers to maintain records about the people who bought their guns. These records had to include the individual's name and address. The 1938 law also prohibited dealers from selling firearms to anyone who had been convicted of a violent felony.

➔ *CASES* V. *U.S.*

A few years after this law was passed, the U.S. Court of Appeals heard a case that would examine the boundaries of the new firearm laws. *Cases* v. *U.S.* (1942) tested the notion that *U.S.* v. *Miller* said an individual could own a weapon if it was one that was used by the military.

The case began when convicted felon Jose Cases Velazquez was arrested while carrying a handgun. This placed him in violation of the Federal Firearms Act. But Cases thought that the ruling in *U.S.* v. *Miller* allowed him to have the gun since it could be used in a militia. His case went before the Supreme Court.

The Court ruled against him. The justices said that although this particular handgun might be used in a military setting, Cases was not using it

Guns & Ammo is a magazine for gun enthusiasts. On their **Guns & Ammo: 2nd Amendment** Web page, you can browse an archive of articles designed to help gun owners deal with Second Amendment issues they encounter in everyday life.

this way. The weapon, therefore, was not contributing to the maintenance of a militia.

The Court went on to say that since "some sort of military use seems to have been found for almost any modern lethal weapon," the ruling in *U.S.* v. *Miller* was meant to be general, not specific.[17] Consequently, Cases had no protection from the Second Amendment ruling, and his possession of a firearm could be regulated by law.[18] Other decisions have followed this same line of thought.

5 THE SECOND AMENDMENT IN COURT: 1960–PRESENT

he 1934 and 1938 gun laws seemed to control gun crime for many decades. Then, in the 1960s, gun violence became an issue again.

Although the Fourteenth Amendment had guaranteed full citizenship rights to all people, some states still discriminated against people of color by keeping them segregated from whites. In the South, for instance, laws kept black people from eating in the same restaurants as white people. In the Southwest, Mexican Americans were not allowed to shop in some stores or live in some neighborhoods.

Tired of unequal treatment, thousands of people protested, demanding equal rights. Many marched in the streets, infiltrated "whites only" businesses, and demanded change. This sometimes led to violence.

At the same time, United States society was struggling with other issues. There was widespread anger over poverty in America. The United States was involved in an unpopular war in Vietnam. The use of illegal drugs became common and controversial.

Civil Rights leader Martin Luther King, Jr., was killed by gunfire in 1968. Senator Robert Kennedy was shot and killed the same year. The deaths of these two leaders renewed efforts to try to stem gun violence in the United States.

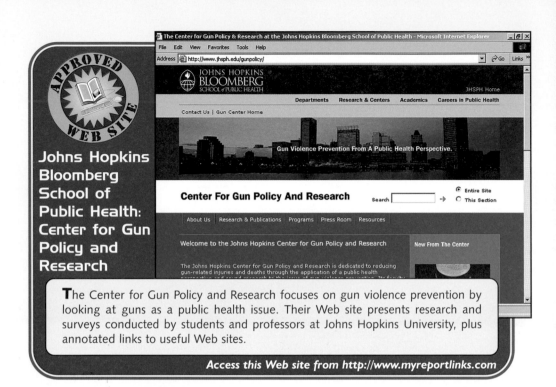

Johns Hopkins
Bloomberg
School of
Public Health:
Center for Gun
Policy and
Research

The Center for Gun Policy and Research focuses on gun violence prevention by looking at guns as a public health issue. Their Web site presents research and surveys conducted by students and professors at Johns Hopkins University, plus annotated links to useful Web sites.

Access this Web site from http://www.myreportlinks.com

Crime rates were high. All of this discontent led to riots, and the riots led to bloody encounters between citizens and police. National Guard units were often called upon to help maintain order.

Furthermore, three national leaders were assassinated by guns during the decade. The first was President John F. Kennedy in 1963. In 1968, civil rights leader Martin Luther King, Jr., was murdered. Later that same year, Senator and presidential candidate Robert F. Kennedy was killed.

➔THE OMNIBUS CRIME CONTROL ACT OF 1968

In an attempt to slow the violence, Congress passed several more gun laws. The Omnibus

Crime Control Act of 1968 established categories of people who could not own guns. Among them were all felons, minors, and illegal drug users.

The Crime Control Act also said that no one could own certain kinds of weapons. Particular handguns, semi-automatic rifles, and machine guns were now illegal in the United States.

In addition, the 1968 laws required more gun sellers than ever before to be licensed. The act said that these gun dealers had to keep thorough records that included each gun's serial number. (The new law also mandated that serial numbers be placed on guns.) This would help law enforcement officers identify the owners of specific guns.

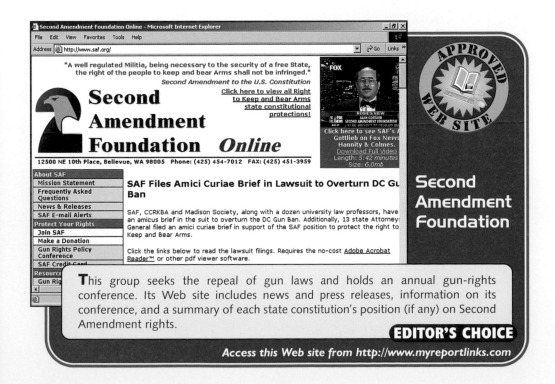

This group seeks the repeal of gun laws and holds an annual gun-rights conference. Its Web site includes news and press releases, information on its conference, and a summary of each state constitution's position (if any) on Second Amendment rights.

EDITOR'S CHOICE

Access this Web site from http://www.myreportlinks.com

Furthermore, the law made gun dealers' records available to federal officials.

→STATES AND GUN CONTROL

Some states took further steps to restrict firearms. New Jersey, for instance, imposed even more limitations on gun ownership.

Not everyone was happy with the new restrictions. In 1968, a New Jersey group decided to test the state's authority to outlaw guns. Among the group were two gun dealers, a company that promoted gun sports, and three members of a gun club. One of them was L. Arthur Burton.

Burton and the others filed a complaint in state court saying that New Jersey's gun laws violated their Second Amendment rights. Arthur J. Sills, New Jersey's attorney general, would defend the state's gun laws. The case, *Burton* v. *Sills* (1968), never went beyond state court.

The New Jersey State Supreme Court ruled against Burton. Like the Supreme Court's ruling in *U.S.* v. *Miller* (1939) decades earlier, the New Jersey court said that the right to bear arms only applied to organized state militias. It said that the Second Amendment was not designed to guarantee a personal liberty. The purpose of the Second Amendment was to guarantee a right to a state government.[1]

Therefore, said the court, New Jersey could make any laws it wanted about guns, as long as they did not interfere with the state's ability to raise a militia. Still not satisfied, the group asked the Supreme Court to review the case. The Court refused, saying there was no substantial federal question to be decided.[2]

Actually, though, the refusal ended up deciding the outcome of the case. By not hearing the case, the Court was saying that New Jersey's gun laws were better left to the lower courts to decide. This reaffirmed that states had the legal right to regulate the sale of guns.

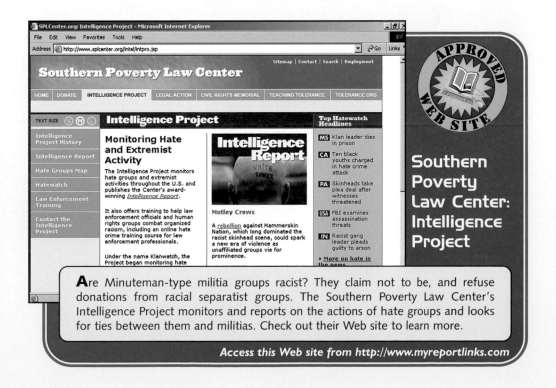

Are Minuteman-type militia groups racist? They claim not to be, and refuse donations from racial separatist groups. The Southern Poverty Law Center's Intelligence Project monitors and reports on the actions of hate groups and looks for ties between them and militias. Check out their Web site to learn more.

Access this Web site from http://www.myreportlinks.com

QUILICI V. VILLAGE OF MORTON GROVE

The case of *Quilici* v. *Village of Morton Grove* (1982) came to a similar end. It began in the small Illinois town of Morton Grove. In 1981, Morton Grove banned the possession of all handguns by private citizens. Handgun owners were required to turn their guns in to the police. Guns for recreational use had to be stored at gun clubs.

People who supported an individual's right to bear arms believed the new law violated the Second Amendment. Victor D. Quilici challenged the law in state court. The case was then combined with similar cases and moved to a federal court.

The court ruled for the town, saying that the Second Amendment does not apply to states or local governments. Quilici then asked the Supreme Court to hear the case. It refused. Once again, its precedent was *U.S.* v. *Miller*.[3]

The precedent set in *U.S.* v. *Miller* has stopped other cases from being heard by the Supreme Court. Many lower courts have used the advice and logic given in the ruling's opinion to guide them. Most courts have ruled in accordance with the *U.S.* v. *Miller* philosophy that the Second Amendment is about a collective right to bear arms.

THE MCCLURE-VOLKMER ACT

In 1986, Congress passed the McClure-Volkmer Act. This law eased restrictions on gun sellers by creating a new category of gun dealers. These were people who sold guns as a hobby, not to earn a living. The new law said that hobby dealers did not have to check the background of their buyers.

→PRIVATE MILITIAS

At about the same time, groups with special interests were forming militias outside the government. These organizations were often founded by individuals with beliefs different from mainstream society.

Part of the Treasury Department, this **Firearms Program: Bureau of Alcohol, Tobacco, Firearms & Explosives** agency Web page provides information on firearms licensing, gun-related crime, community outreach, and more.

Many of the groups were racist. Some groups were against a strong national government. They believed that there should be no government beyond the county level. Some groups refused to pay taxes. Others were radical right Christian organizations. Still others were opposed to environmental regulations.

People in many of these groups often feared that the government would intrude into their lives. To protect themselves from this, they felt they needed to be armed. So they stockpiled weapons and ammunition. They believed this right was guaranteed to them in the Second Amendment.

Citizen groups with large stores of weaponry often alarmed neighbors who were not a part of the group. Privately held weapon caches also worried law enforcement agents. Many believed the weapons were either illegal or had been obtained illegally.

The Department of Justice and Bureau of Alcohol, Tobacco, Firearms and Explosives was criticized by some people for the way it handled the situation involving the Branch Davidian members in Waco, Texas.

At times, local authorities asked federal officials to help them contain or confront a group. Two federal agencies were often called upon to do so. One was the Federal Bureau of Investigation (FBI). Its job is to deal with crimes against the government. The other was the Bureau of Alcohol, Tobacco, Firearms and Explosives (ATF). Its job is to enforce gun regulations.

Interaction between government authorities and citizen groups sometimes led to conflict. One of the best known and most tragic of these was the 1993 confrontation between the federal government and the Branch Davidians.

➔THE BRANCH DAVIDIANS

The Branch Davidians were a small religious group headed by David Koresh. They lived in quiet isolation just outside the town of Waco, Texas. Authorities became concerned about the group's activities when former members came to them saying that people in the group had abused them. Officials were also troubled by reports of large stores of weapons and ammunition being kept on the Davidian compound.

In February 1993, the ATF approached the group's headquarters. When Davidian members began shooting at them, the FBI was called in to help. This began a fifty-one-day standoff. Eventually, the FBI stormed the compound. As they did, some people on the inside set their buildings on fire. By the time the conflict ended, more than eighty Davidians and four federal agents were dead.

Many people criticized the government's actions in the raid. They believed poor judgment and a rush to action led to unnecessary deaths. Some of the loudest criticism came from militia groups. They believed the government had infringed on several rights set forth in the Constitution. This, they said, was exactly why small groups had to arm themselves. They believed the Second Amendment gave them the right to do so.

Yet the Supreme Court's majority decisions in *Presser* v. *Illinois* (1886) and *U.S.* v. *Miller* (1939) clearly stated that special interest groups had

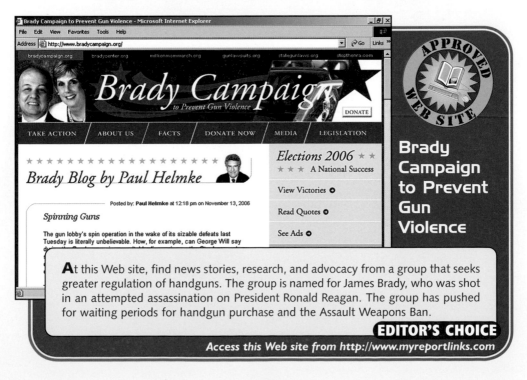

Brady Campaign to Prevent Gun Violence

At this Web site, find news stories, research, and advocacy from a group that seeks greater regulation of handguns. The group is named for James Brady, who was shot in an attempted assassination on President Ronald Reagan. The group has pushed for waiting periods for handgun purchase and the Assault Weapons Ban.

EDITOR'S CHOICE

Access this Web site from http://www.myreportlinks.com

The Assault Weapons Ban, passed in 1994, outlawed large-scale assault weapons such as ones that used feeding devices like this one. This particular magazine was for military use.

DO NOT LOAD OVER 300 RNDS. IN THIS TRAY

START HERE - CAPACITY 500 RNDS.

no right to build a private militia. Together the rulings defined militias as being government-approved groups that states could regulate as they saw fit.

⊜Gun Law in the 1990s

By the early 1990s, more firearm laws had been passed by Congress. The manufacture of explosives had been restricted, and armor-piercing ammunition was made illegal. Firearms that could not be "seen" by metal detectors were also made illegal.

Several states had also been passing gun laws, many of which expanded firearm rights. This reflected people's concern with their own safety. Gun violence in America was again on the rise. Some people felt they needed their own firearms to protect themselves against criminals.

Florida passed a law allowing people to carry concealed weapons. Other states soon followed.

In addition, some states passed what became known as "Make My Day" laws. These laws were made with the belief that people had an absolute right to be safe in their homes. A "Make My Day" law allowed a house's occupant to use deadly force if necessary to stop any intruder who might commit a crime.

Other people sought a different solution to gun crime. They believed far too many criminals had access to guns. These people thought federal gun

By the late 1990s, over 5 million people attended gun shows in the United States.

The
Coalition to
Stop Gun
Violence

Coalition to Stop Gun Violence / Educational Fund to Stop Gun Violence - Microsoft Internet Explorer

File   Edit   View   Favorites   Tools   Help

Address ᵊ http://www.csgv.org/   ▾   Go   Links »

| Take Action | Donate | Issues & Campaigns | Get Involved | News | Research |

THE COALITION TO STOP GUN VIOLENCE
THE EDUCATIONAL FUND TO STOP GUN VIOLENCE
Organizing for Progressive Gun Laws Since 1974.

What's New

2006 ELECTIONS DEMONSTRATE LIMITS OF GUN LOBBY'S INFLUENCE

NRA-backed candidates lose in key House, Senate and governor races

Washington, DC – On November 7, candidates endorsed by the National Rifle Association fared poorly in election races across the country, as Democrats regained control of the House of Representatives and Senate.

Read the rest of the release.

make a donation
you can help make a difference.

sign up for updates

[   ]   sign up →
enter your email address to
receive the latest news.

new to the issue?

THE CSGV BLOG:

This coalition includes religious, labor, medical, educational, and civic groups. It lobbies state and federal lawmakers. Its Web site includes information on issues and campaigns covering topics such as assault weapons and the gun show loophole, news and press releases, research on guns and gun violence, and more.

Access this Web site from http://www.myreportlinks.com

control laws needed tightening. One was James Brady.

Brady was President Ronald Reagan's press secretary in 1981. That year he was inadvertently shot when someone tried to assassinate President Reagan. He had survived, but his injury left him permanently disabled.

After the shooting, Brady and his wife, Sarah, became devoted activists for gun control. They worked to get Congress to pass gun laws that became known as the Brady Bill.

⊖THE BRADY BILL

The Brady Handgun Violence Prevention Act was passed in 1993. It required a five-day waiting period for anyone who wanted to buy a gun. During this time, law enforcement agencies were required to conduct background checks on individuals to see if they had criminal records.

The waiting time was also meant to be a "cooling down" period. Anyone buying a gun because he or she was angry or depressed would have time to reconsider the idea. If the person was unstable, the waiting period might give friends, family, or law enforcement agents time to intervene.

Another law the Bradys worked for was the Violent Crime Control and Law Enforcement Act. This law was commonly called the Assault Weapons Ban. It would ban the manufacture, sale, and possession of certain kinds of guns known as assault weapons. These were most often semiautomatic firearms.

Semiautomatic guns fire one bullet then instantly load the next bullet. Therefore, several bullets can be fired in rapid succession with no need to cock the weapon between shots. Other weapons that fell into the assault weapon category were rifles with bayonet mounts on them, and grenade launchers.

PASSING THE BAN

In addition, the Assault Weapons Ban would outlaw large capacity ammunition feeding devices known as magazines. Like semi-automatic weapons,

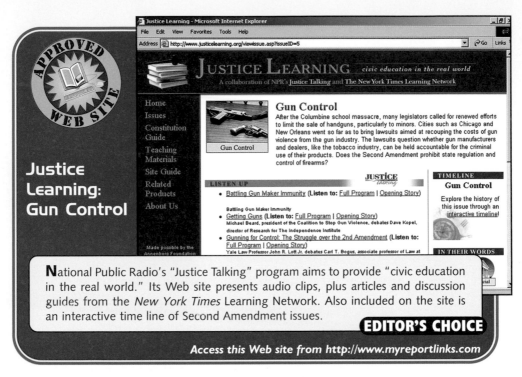

Justice
Learning:
Gun Control

Justice Learning - Microsoft Internet Explorer

File   Edit   View   Favorites   Tools   Help

Address http://www.justicelearning.org/viewissue.asp?issueID=5   Go   Links

JUSTICE LEARNING   *civic education in the real world*
A collaboration of NPR's Justice Talking and The New York Times Learning Network

Home
Issues
Constitution Guide
Teaching Materials
Site Guide
Related Products
About Us

Made possible by the Annenberg Foundation

Gun Control

After the Columbine school massacre, many legislators called for renewed efforts to limit the sale of handguns, particularly to minors. Cities such as Chicago and New Orleans went so far as to bring lawsuits aimed at recouping the costs of gun violence from the gun industry. The lawsuits question whether gun manufacturers and dealers, like the tobacco industry, can be held accountable for the criminal use of their products. Does the Second Amendment prohibit state regulation and control of firearms?

Gun Control

JUSTICE *talking*

LISTEN UP

• Battling Gun Maker Immunity (**Listen to:** Full Program | Opening Story)

   Battling Gun Maker Immunity
• Getting Guns (**Listen to:** Full Program | Opening Story)
   Michael Beard, president of the Coalition to Stop Gun Violence, debates Dave Kopel, director of Research for The Independence Institute
• Gunning for Control: The Struggle over the 2nd Amendment (**Listen to:** Full Program | Opening Story)
   Yale Law Professor John R. Lott Jr. debates Carl T. Bogus, associate professor of Law at

TIMELINE
Gun Control
Explore the history of this issue through an interactive timeline!

IN THEIR WORDS

National Public Radio's "Justice Talking" program aims to provide "civic education in the real world." Its Web site presents audio clips, plus articles and discussion guides from the *New York Times* Learning Network. Also included on the site is an interactive time line of Second Amendment issues.

EDITOR'S CHOICE

Access this Web site from http://www.myreportlinks.com

their purpose was to increase the number of bullets a weapon could fire in a short time.

Supporters of the ban argued that there was no legal use for these kinds of weapons outside of the military. They pointed out that the Assault Weapons Ban would not prohibit guns used in hunting or recreational activities.

Most law enforcement groups heartily endorsed the ban. Many reported "that semi-automatic [firearms] had become the 'weapon of choice' for drug traffickers, gangs, and paramilitary extremist groups."[4]

The ban was passed in 1994 for a ten-year period. At the end of the ten years, it could be renewed with Congress's approval.

U.S. v. LOPEZ

By 1995, federal laws defined who could own guns, who could sell guns, and the kinds of firearms that could be owned. Some people thought that these restrictions went beyond the limits of the Constitution. Many wondered how many gun laws the federal government could make and still not violate the Second Amendment.

In 1995, the Supreme Court heard a case that would test this. In *U.S.* v. *Lopez,* a high school student was found guilty of having taken a gun to school. Lopez had violated the Gun-Free School Zones Act. This federal law said an individual could not possess a gun within 1,000 feet of a school. Lopez was found guilty, and his case was appealed to the Supreme Court.

The Supreme Court ruled with Lopez. It said the law he was arrested for breaking was not valid. The ruling did not mean that the Supreme Court approved of students taking guns to school. It meant that the Court did not agree that the Commerce Clause gave Congress the authority to make the school-zone law. The law, said the Court, had nothing to do with business. Therefore, outlawing guns in school zones was a state matter, not a federal matter.[5]

GAPS IN THE GUN LAWS

Gun control remained an issue of concern throughout the 1990s. Many people were alarmed by how many children had easy access to guns. One study indicated that over 40 percent of American households with children had guns. Many times these weapons were left loaded and unlocked.[6]

Several groups fought to make guns safer. They urged gun makers to equip their weapons with child safety locks and to make triggers harder to pull.

People were also concerned with gun dealers who either ignored gun laws or found a way around them. Many believed there were too many gaps, or loopholes, in the law. These loopholes allowed people to follow the law but still sell weapons to criminals.

Gun control advocates noted that guns could be purchased legally on the Internet or through newspaper advertisements without a buyer having a background check. Most alarming of all was what became known as the gun show loophole.

By the late 1990s, about five thousand gun shows were being held across America each year. These brought in an annual attendance of 5 million people.[7] And because of the McClure-Volkmer Act, any one of these people could buy a gun from a hobby dealer without a background check.

LAWSUITS AGAINST CORPORATIONS

While some people worked to close the loopholes, others fought for stricter gun control through lawsuits. In Florida, for example, Deborah Kitchen took K-Mart Corporation to court. A salesperson there had sold her ex-boyfriend a gun while he was intoxicated. He had taken the weapon and shot her. Kitchen survived and then sued K-Mart for more than $11 million. The Florida Supreme Court upheld the *Kitchen* v. *K-Mart Corporation* (1997) verdict.[8]

Not all lawsuits were as successful. In 1998, New Orleans became the first city to file a lawsuit against gun makers and dealers. Mayor Marc M. Morial sued Smith and Wesson and fourteen other handgun makers. Morial claimed that his city had suffered harm because gun manufacturers had failed to implement safer gun designs. These designs would have prevented unauthorized use of the guns by children and others.

This case never made it to court. In 1999, the Louisiana legislature made a law prohibiting such lawsuits. The city asked the state Supreme Court to rule on the legality of the law. The court upheld the law, so the case was not heard. Determined city officials asked the Supreme Court to hear the case. It refused, but gave no reason why.

Soon after, Chicago filed a lawsuit against gun manufacturers, distributors, and dealers. In the *City of Chicago* v. *Beretta U.S.A. Corporation* (1998), Chicago asked for $433 million in damages. The city charged that the gun industry's

During the decade between 1997 and 2007 Americans were shocked by a number of school shootings. Among the questions asked were, How were these guns getting into the hands of young people?

reckless behavior kept Chicago criminals with a steady supply of guns. It estimated that as a result, the city's taxpayers had spent $433 million on medical and emergency services.

After a series of court decisions, the case ended up in the Illinois Supreme Court. It dismissed the case.[9]

⮕ THE DEBATE CONTINUES

By 1998, the five-day waiting period portion of the Brady Bill had been replaced by the National Instant Criminal Background Check System (NICS). This computerized database told gun dealers almost instantly if someone had been convicted of a crime that prohibited him or her from owning a firearm.

The NICS check had to be made before any federally licensed firearms dealers sold a gun. Many people were glad this process took only a few minutes to complete. Others felt that a waiting period was a sensible way to reduce gun violence brought on by sudden emotion.

During the late 1990s, gun violence was making headlines once more. This time it was because of a series of school shootings. One of the worst occurred in Littleton, Colorado, in 1999. Two students went on a shooting rampage at their Denver-area high school and murdered twelve students and a teacher. The Columbine High School killings shocked the nation.

The event sparked another national debate about gun laws. Many people wondered if federal gun laws were strict enough. Others argued that in spite of gun violence, the Second Amendment said there could be no laws against private gun ownership.

U.S. v. EMERSON

One case soon tested the limits of the United States Supreme Court's Second Amendment beliefs. Sacha Emerson was divorcing her husband. She had a restraining order against him. This is a legal order that says one person is not to come near another person. Federal law prohibits anyone under a restraining order to carry a firearm. Dr. Timothy Joe Emerson then threatened his wife with a gun, and he was indicted for illegal possession of a weapon.

But the judge who heard the case ruled in favor of Dr. Timothy Joe Emerson. He maintained that the law that kept him from having a weapon was unconstitutional under the Second Amendment. In his ruling, the judge said, "A textual analysis of the Second Amendment supports an individual right to bear arms."[10]

This ruling was in direct contradiction to U.S. v. Miller. So the United States government appealed the decision. In 2001, the U.S. Court of Appeals reversed the original decision. The

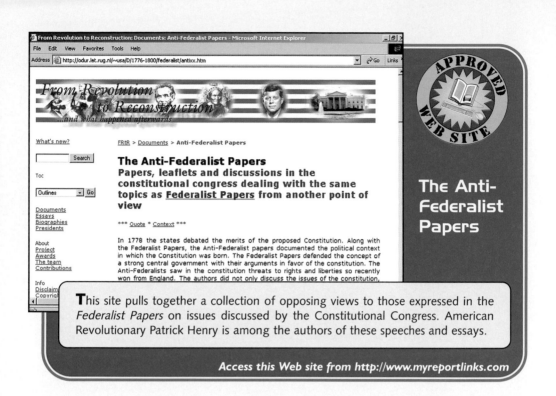

This site pulls together a collection of opposing views to those expressed in the *Federalist Papers* on issues discussed by the Constitutional Congress. American Revolutionary Patrick Henry is among the authors of these speeches and essays.

Access this Web site from http://www.myreportlinks.com

appeals court reinstated the charges against Emerson and said that the restriction was constitutional. This second ruling seemed to agree with *U.S.* v. *Miller.*

⊖ STATE RIGHTS

The Supreme Court again followed *U.S.* v. *Miller* in 2001. That year it refused to hear *Kasler* v. *Lockyer.* This brought an end to a case that had begun before the federal Assault Weapons Ban had been made. At the time, California had its own laws outlawing the sale of assault weapons. *Kasler* v. *Lockyer* challenged the constitutionality of the California law.

When the California Supreme Court ruled the law constitutional, the case was appealed to the United States Supreme Court. The Supreme Court refused to hear the case, making it seem as though it would not interfere with a state's ability to make gun laws.

➡THE END OF THE ASSAULT WEAPON'S BAN

In 1993, about 580,000 crimes had been committed with firearms. By 2003, that number had decreased to around 347,000.[11] Some people attributed the drop to background checks and the Assault Weapons Ban.

But the ten-year limit on the Assault Weapons Ban was nearing an end. As its expiration date grew near, supporters realized that Congress was not going to ask for an extension. They asked President George W. Bush to urge lawmakers to extend the bill. He did not. The deadline passed and the Assault Weapons Ban expired in 2004.

THE FUTURE OF THE SECOND AMENDMENT

6

S upreme Court rulings have given legal scholars two guiding principles in interpreting the Second Amendment. The first is the Supreme Court's belief that the Second Amendment gives states the right to maintain a militia. *U.S.* v. *Miller* (1939) and *Presser* v. *Illinois* (1886) make this clear. According to the Supreme Court, the Second Amendment was written to protect militias that are created by state governments.

The Supreme Court's second guiding principle is that the Second Amendment protects a public right, not an individual right. *U.S.* v. *Miller* has set the precedent for this belief. Consequently, the Second Amendment is only one of a few amendments in the Bill of Rights that has not been incorporated against the states.[1]

By not incorporating the Second Amendment, the Court is saying that the Constitution does not give an individual the right to own a weapon. This has had the effect of allowing states to regulate firearms as they choose.

These two guiding principles have set the constitutional boundaries for today's gun laws. Federal, state, and local laws that regulate guns must fall within these boundaries. In practice, the Supreme Court has found laws about owning firearms constitutional. It supports laws for and against carrying concealed weapons. It has allowed laws requiring the registration of firearms and the licensing of firearms dealers. Furthermore, the Supreme Court has said it is constitutional to prohibit certain people from owning firearms.

DISAGREEMENT WITH *U.S.* v. *MILLER*

Yet not everyone agrees with the Supreme Court's interpretation of the Second Amendment. For example, there are those who believe the Court's ruling in *U.S.* v. *Miller* was incorrect.[2] They say the Court was wrong to say the Second Amendment is about a collective right to bear arms.

Others think the opinion in the ruling has been misinterpreted. They do not think the opinion supports a collective rights view of the amendment.[3] They believe an open-minded review of the opinion would lead many people to see it as an individual rights ruling.

Groups and individuals who do not like the *U.S.* v. *Miller* precedent keep taking gun cases to

Supreme Court rulings have given states the ability to regulate the ownership of firearms.

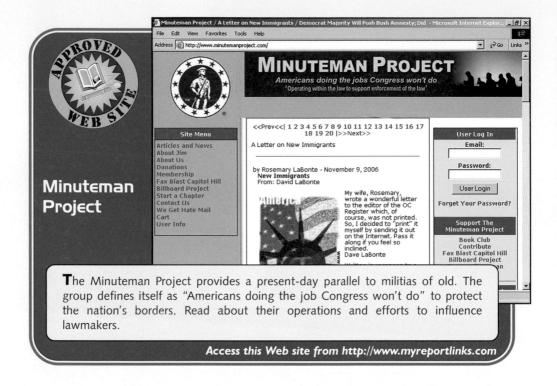

Minuteman Project

MINUTEMAN PROJECT
Americans doing the jobs Congress won't do
'Operating within the law to support enforcement of the law'

<<Prev<< | 1 2 3 4 5 6 7 8 9 10 11 12 13 14 15 16 17 18 19 20 |>>Next>>

A Letter on New Immigrants
_____

by Rosemary LaBonte - November 9, 2006
New Immigrants
From: David LaBonte

My wife, Rosemary, wrote a wonderful letter to the editor of the OC Register which, of course, was not printed. So, I decided to "print" it myself by sending it out on the Internet. Pass it along if you feel so inclined.
Dave LaBonte

Site Menu
Articles and News
About Jim
About Us
Donations
Membership
Fax Blast Capitol Hill
Billboard Project
Start a Chapter
Contact Us
We Get Hate Mail
Cart
User Info

User Log In
Email:
Password:
User Login
Forget Your Password?

Support The Minuteman Project
Book Club
Contribute
Fax Blast Capitol Hill
Billboard Project

The Minuteman Project provides a present-day parallel to militias of old. The group defines itself as "Americans doing the job Congress won't do" to protect the nation's borders. Read about their operations and efforts to influence lawmakers.

Access this Web site from http://www.myreportlinks.com

court. They hope that one day a ruling will overturn the Supreme Court's 1939 decision.

Some of those people belong to militia groups. Today there are active militias in many states. Several groups are well known to the public and law authorities. Others, though, are rarely seen or heard from.

But not all of the people who oppose the Supreme Court's collective rights rulings are people with extreme views. Thousands of ordinary citizens believe the Second Amendment was written to protect every individual's right to own a gun. They believe that any gun laws—federal, state, or local—encroach on this freedom.

At least one Supreme Court justice may feel the same. In a recent opinion, Justice Clarence Thomas noted that individual rights theorists have gathered evidence to suggest that "the right to keep and bear arms" is referring to a personal right.[4]

➔The NRA

Many people who believe in the individual right to bear arms belong to organizations that promote gun ownership. One of the largest is the National Rifle Association (NRA). The NRA has a membership of 4 million people. Among them are gun owners, gun sellers, and gun makers.

The NRA is a powerful organization. It hires lobbyists who work to keep gun laws at a minimum. The job of a lobbyist is to influence lawmakers.

Lobbyists do this in a number of ways. Sometimes they get like-minded citizens to contact legislators about laws they want made or repealed. Sometimes lobbyists help people with certain views get elected to office. Lobbyists also appeal directly to legislators.

➔The Million Mom March

Gun control advocates are just as committed to their cause. They believe that guns are too easy to obtain in America. Many point to the fact that more people in the United States die by gun violence than in any other nation.[5]

Million Mom March Chapters - Microsoft Internet Explorer

File   Edit   View   Favorites   Tools   Help

Address http://www.millionmommarch.com/

bradycampaign.org | bradycenter.org | millionmommarch.org | gunlawsuits.org | stopthenra.com | stategunlaws.org

MILLION MOM MARCH chapters
of the Brady Campaign to Prevent Gun Violence

sensible gun laws, safe kids

about us | action | learn | awards | donate | shop

join us! get involved!

Select Your State:

Elections 2006 ★ ★
★ ★ ★ A National Success

View Victories ●

Read Quotes ●

See Ads ●

...ate an America where all people are safe from gun violence ...eighborhoods, schools, and places of work and worship.
read more...

...ocal chapter!

The **Million Mom March** started as a march on Washington, D.C., in 2000 to promote sensible gun laws. It is now an affiliate of the Brady Campaign and consists of seventy-five local chapters that strive to promote gun safety and awareness. Learn more about the group on their Web site.

Donna Dees-Thomases was so concerned about gun violence that she organized a rally in Washington, D.C., on Mother's Day in 2000. That day nearly eight hundred thousand people gathered to tell lawmakers they wanted stricter gun control laws.

Since then, Dees-Thomases has created a national organization called the Million Mom March. This group supports local and state groups that work toward ending various loopholes in gun laws. Most members are dismayed by the fact that over eleven thousand Americans are murdered each year with a firearm.[6]

➔GUN REGISTRATION

Many people who oppose gun control laws are just as concerned about gun violence. However, they do not think that more gun laws will end violence. They believe a criminal's fear of being met with a gun will. They also think that if current gun laws were strongly enforced, gun violence would decrease. Finally, those opposed to more gun laws believe strong safety education programs would reduce unnecessary deaths.

However, gun control advocates say safety education is not enough. They want laws that require guns to have locks that children cannot undo. They urge gun makers to continue developing other safety technologies as well. For example, guns with locks that release only when someone with a specific finger or palm print is holding a gun.

Furthermore, gun control advocates want the government to require firearm owners to register their guns. They believe this is nothing more restrictive than the government's requirement that citizens license and register cars. Registration would allow law enforcement authorities to trace weapons used in crimes.

Yet some people are deeply opposed to registration. They believe registration is a government's first step in disarming the people.[7] Those with this view feel that a central registration system would

Citizens in favor of gun control oftentimes support the idea of forcing people to register their guns. This way, if a gun is used inappropriately it would be easier to track who may be responsible.

make it easy for the federal government to find gun owners and take their guns.

→ GUNS AND TERRORISTS

In recent years, gun control supporters have talked about a new reason to tighten gun laws. They say that terrorists around the world come to the United States to buy guns and ammunition. Loopholes in United States law make it easy for them to find and buy enough firearms to create an arsenal of assault weapons. According to a report from the Brady Center to Prevent Gun Violence, terrorists see the United States as "the Great Gun Bazaar."[8]

→ THE BRADY CENTER

The Brady Center is the largest organization in the United States today working to prevent gun violence. It was founded in 1974 by Dr. Mark Borinsky, himself a victim of gun violence. Borinsky named his organization the National Council to Control Handguns (NCCH). Since the mid-1980s, James and Sarah Brady devoted so many hours to the organization that it was renamed in their honor in 2001.

Today the Brady Center lobbies to get what many call "sensible" gun laws passed. This includes getting the Assault Weapons Ban and waiting period for gun purchases reinstated. The

Center also works to increase regulation of the gun industry. Finally, the organization gives legal support to victims of gun violence.

→GUN CONTROL LAWS IN THE FUTURE

Should lawmakers try to make society safer by creating more gun laws? There are powerful forces on both sides of the debate. At the core of the discussion is the meaning of the Second Amendment.

Is the Second Amendment about an individual right to bear arms? Or is it speaking of a collective right that applies only to the governments of the states? Future gun laws will depend on how people in power view the Second Amendment.

Those people include legislators. If lawmakers believe the Second Amendment is about a collective right to bear arms, they may be willing to make more laws regulating guns. If they believe it is about an individual's right, they may reject gun control proposals or even repeal current laws.

The president, too, will affect future gun laws. He or she is an influential force in suggesting what laws legislators should make or repeal.

The president plays another important role in determining the future of Second Amendment issues. It is the president who chooses Supreme Court justices when there is an opening on the Court.

Many presidents have been careful to choose justices who share their ideas about the meaning of the Constitution. Because it is the justices who decide whether or not new laws are constitutional, choosing the right justice can determine whether a president is able to get certain laws passed.

Since 1939, the Supreme Court has used the case *U.S.* v. *Miller* as its precedent to interpret Second Amendment issues. However, there is no requirement for it to continue to do so.

Future justices may hold different views as to the meaning of the Second Amendment. If so, they may rule differently on gun cases. Their new rulings may change the current boundaries of gun law.

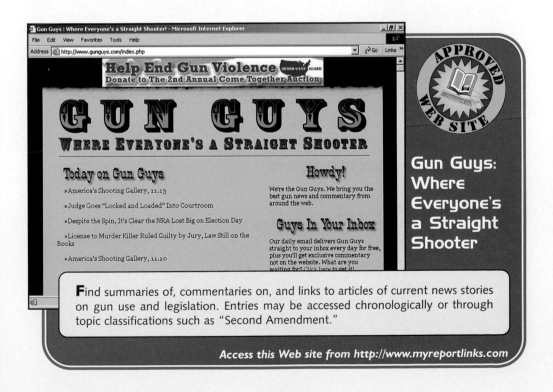

Find summaries of, commentaries on, and links to articles of current news stories on gun use and legislation. Entries may be accessed chronologically or through topic classifications such as "Second Amendment."

Access this Web site from http://www.myreportlinks.com

Proponents of a citizen's right to bear arms and gun control advocates agree that it is important to treat guns responsibly so they do not end up in the wrong hands.

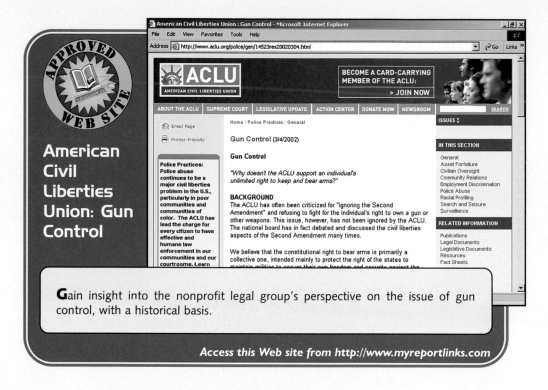

American
Civil
Liberties
Union: Gun
Control

American Civil Liberties Union : Gun Control - Microsoft Internet Explorer

File   Edit   View   Favorites   Tools   Help

Address http://www.aclu.org/police/gen/14523res20020304.html

ACLU
AMERICAN CIVIL LIBERTIES UNION

BECOME A CARD-CARRYING
MEMBER OF THE ACLU:
> JOIN NOW

ABOUT THE ACLU | SUPREME COURT | LEGISLATIVE UPDATE | ACTION CENTER | DONATE NOW | NEWSROOM

SEARCH

Email Page   Home : Police Practices : General

Printer-Friendly   Gun Control (3/4/2002)

Police Practices: **Gun Control**
Police abuse
continues to be a   *"Why doesn't the ACLU support an individual's*
major civil liberties   *unlimited right to keep and bear arms?"*
problem in the U.S.,
particularly in poor   **BACKGROUND**
communities and   The ACLU has often been criticized for "ignoring the Second
communities of   Amendment" and refusing to fight for the individual's right to own a gun or
color. The ACLU has   other weapons. This issue, however, has not been ignored by the ACLU.
lead the charge for   The national board has in fact debated and discussed the civil liberties
every citizen to have   aspects of the Second Amendment many times.
effective and
humane law   We believe that the constitutional right to bear arms is primarily a
enforcement in our   collective one, intended mainly to protect the right of the states to
communities and our
courtrooms. Learn

ISSUES

IN THIS SECTION

General
Asset Forfeiture
Civilian Oversight
Community Relations
Employment Discrimination
Police Abuse
Racial Profiling
Search and Seizure
Surveillance

RELATED INFORMATION

Publications
Legal Documents
Legislative Documents
Resources
Fact Sheets

Gain insight into the nonprofit legal group's perspective on the issue of gun control, with a historical basis.

Access this Web site from http://www.myreportlinks.com

→VOTERS AND THE SECOND AMENDMENT

The people with the most power to determine Second Amendment law are the voters. They will choose the lawmakers who make the laws. They will elect the president who will suggest the laws and perhaps appoint a Supreme Court justice who will interpret laws.

Voters who want to affect the law will first have to think about their own interpretation of the Second Amendment. Is it about a collective right to own firearms? Or is it about an individual right?

Several factors may play into their Second Amendment analysis. For example, how important is the original intent of the nation's founders to how the Constitution is interpreted today? How important are society's current needs when deciding on the meaning of the Constitution?

Voters will also have to weigh their desire for a safe society with their desire to own guns. They will have to determine how or if gun regulation can strike a balance between the two.

Finally, people will have to decide which lawmakers best represent their feelings. Those who choose people carefully and help them become elected will have the best chance of having their opinions heard.

Ultimately, then, it is tomorrow's voters who will decide on the future of Second Amendment laws. This means that future gun laws may very well depend on you.

The Constitution of the United States

The text of the Constitution is presented here. All words are given their modern spelling and capitalization. Brackets [ ] indicate parts that have been changed or set aside by amendments.

Preamble

We the People of the United States, in Order to form a more perfect Union, establish Justice, insure domestic Tranquillity, provide for the common defence, promote the general Welfare, and secure the Blessings of Liberty to ourselves and our Posterity, do ordain and establish this Constitution for the United States of America.

Article I
The Legislative Branch

Section 1. All legislative powers herein granted shall be vested in a Congress of the United States, which shall consist of a Senate and House of Representatives.

The House of Representatives

Section 2. The House of Representatives shall be composed of members chosen every second year by the people of the several states, and the electors in each state shall have the qualifications requisite for electors of the most numerous branch of the state legislature.

No person shall be a Representative who shall not have attained to the age of twenty five years, and been seven years a citizen of the United States, and who shall not, when elected, be an inhabitant of that state in which he shall be chosen.

Representatives and direct taxes shall be apportioned among the several states which may be included within this union, according to their respective numbers, [which shall be determined by adding to the whole number of free persons, including those bound to service for a term of years, and excluding Indians not taxed, three fifths of all other persons]. The actual Enumeration shall be made within three years after the first meeting of the Congress of the United States, and within every subsequent term of ten years, in such manner as they shall by law direct. The number of Representatives shall not exceed one for every thirty thousand, but each state shall have at least one Representative; [and until such enumeration shall be made, the state of New Hampshire shall be entitled to chuse three, Massachusetts eight, Rhode Island and Providence Plantations one, Connecticut five, New York six, New Jersey four, Pennsylvania eight, Delaware one, Maryland six, Virginia ten, North Carolina five, South Carolina five, and Georgia three].

When vacancies happen in the Representation from any state, the executive authority thereof shall issue writs of election to fill such vacancies.

The House of Representatives shall choose their speaker and other officers; and shall have the sole power of impeachment.

The Senate

Section 3. The Senate of the United States shall be composed of two Senators from each state, [chosen by the legislature thereof,] for six years; and each Senator shall have one vote.

Immediately after they shall be assembled in consequence of the first election, they shall be divided as equally as may be into three classes. The seats of the Senators of the first class shall be vacated at the expiration of the second year, of the second class at the expiration of the fourth year, and the third class at the expiration of the sixth year, so that one third may be chosen every second year; [and if vacancies happen by resignation, or otherwise, during the recess of the legislature of any state, the executive thereof may make temporary appointments until the next meeting of the legislature, which shall then fill such vacancies].

No person shall be a Senator who shall not have attained to the age of thirty years, and been nine years a citizen of the United States and who shall not, when elected, be an inhabitant of that state for which he shall be chosen.

The Vice President of the United States shall be President of the Senate, but shall have no vote, unless they be equally divided.

The Senate shall choose their other officers, and also a President pro tempore, in the absence of the Vice President, or when he shall exercise the office of President of the United States.

The Senate shall have the sole power to try all impeachments. When sitting for that purpose, they shall be on oath or affirmation. When the President of the United States is tried, the Chief Justice shall preside: And no person shall be convicted without the concurrence of two thirds of the members present.

Judgment in cases of impeachment shall not extend further than to removal from office, and disqualification to hold and enjoy any office of honor, trust or profit under the United States: but the party convicted shall nevertheless be liable and subject to indictment, trial, judgment and punishment, according to law.

Organization of Congress

Section 4. The times, places and manner of holding elections for Senators and Representatives, shall be prescribed in each state by the legislature thereof; but the Congress may at any time by law make or alter such regulations, [except as to the places of choosing senators].

The Congress shall assemble at least once in every year, [and such meeting shall be on the first Monday in December], unless they shall by law appoint a different day.

Section 5. Each House shall be the judge of the elections, returns and qualifications of its own members, and a majority of each shall constitute a quorum to do business; but a smaller number may adjourn from day to day, and may be authorized to compel the attendance of absent members, in such manner, and under such penalties as each House may provide.

Each House may determine the rules of its proceedings, punish its members for disorderly behavior, and, with the concurrence of two thirds, expel a member.

Each House shall keep a journal of its proceedings, and from time to time publish the same, excepting such parts as may in their judgment require secrecy; and the yeas and nays of the members of either House on any question shall, at the desire of one fifth of those present, be entered on the journal.

Neither House, during the session of Congress, shall, without the consent of the other, adjourn for more than three days, nor to any other place than that in which the two Houses shall be sitting.

Section 6. The Senators and Representatives shall receive a compensation for their services, to be ascertained by law, and paid out of the treasury of the United States. They shall in all cases, except treason, felony and breach of the peace, be privileged from arrest during their attendance at the session of their respective Houses, and in going to and returning from the same; and for any speech or debate in either House, they shall not be questioned in any other place.

No Senator or Representative shall, during the time for which he was elected, be appointed to any civil office under the authority of the United States, which shall have been created, or the emoluments whereof shall have been increased during such time: and no person holding any office under the United States, shall be a member of either House during his continuance in office.

Section 7. All bills for raising revenue shall originate in the House of Representatives; but the Senate may propose or concur with amendments as on other Bills.

Every bill which shall have passed the House of Representatives and the Senate, shall, before it become a law, be presented to the President of the United States; if he approve he shall sign it, but if not he shall return it, with his objections to that House in which it shall have originated, who shall enter the objections at large on their journal, and proceed to reconsider it. If after such reconsideration two thirds of that House shall agree to pass the bill, it shall be sent, together with the objections, to the other House, by which it shall likewise be reconsidered, and if approved by two thirds of that House, it shall become a law. But in all such cases the votes of both Houses shall be determined by yeas and nays, and the names of the persons voting for and against the bill shall be entered on the journal of each House respectively. If any bill shall not be returned by the President within ten days (Sundays excepted) after it shall have been presented to him, the same shall be a law, in like manner as if he had signed it, unless the Congress by their adjournment prevent its return, in which case it shall not be a law.

Every order, resolution, or vote to which the concurrence of the Senate and House of Representatives may be necessary (except on a question of adjournment) shall be presented to the President of the United States; and before the same shall take effect, shall be approved by him, or being disapproved by him, shall be repassed by two thirds of the Senate and House of Representatives, according to the rules and limitations prescribed in the case of a bill.

Powers Granted to Congress
The Congress shall have the power:

Section 8. To lay and collect taxes, duties, imposts and excises, to pay the debts and provide for the common defense and general welfare of the United States; but all duties, imposts and excises shall be uniform throughout the United States;

To borrow money on the credit of the United States;

To regulate commerce with foreign nations, and among the several states, and with the Indian tribes;

To establish a uniform rule of naturalization, and uniform laws on the subject of bankruptcies throughout the United States;

To coin money, regulate the value thereof, and of foreign coin, and fix the standard of weights and measures;

To provide for the punishment of counterfeiting the securities and current coin of the United States;

To establish post offices and post roads;

To promote the progress of science and useful arts, by securing for limited times to authors and inventors the exclusive right to their respective writings and discoveries;

To constitute tribunals inferior to the Supreme Court;

To define and punish piracies and felonies committed on the high seas, and offenses against the law of nations;

To declare war, grant letters of marque and reprisal, and make rules concerning captures on land and water;

To raise and support armies, but no appropriation of money to that use shall be for a longer term than two years;

To provide and maintain a navy;

To make rules for the government and regulation of the land and naval forces;

To provide for calling forth the militia to execute the laws of the union, suppress insurrections and repel invasions;

To provide for organizing, arming, and disciplining, the militia, and for governing such part of them as may be employed in the service of the United States, reserving to the states respectively, the appointment of the officers, and the authority of training the militia according to the discipline prescribed by Congress;

To exercise exclusive legislation in all cases whatsoever, over such District (not exceeding ten miles square) as may, by cession of particular states, and the acceptance of Congress, become the seat of the government of the United States, and to exercise like authority over all places purchased by the consent of the legislature of the state in which the same shall be, for the erection of forts, magazines, arsenals, dockyards, and other needful buildings;—And

To make all laws which shall be necessary and proper for carrying into execution the foregoing powers, and all other powers vested by this Constitution in the government of the United States, or in any depart-ment or officer thereof.

Powers Forbidden to Congress

Section 9. The migration or importation of such persons as any of the states now existing shall think proper to admit, shall not be prohibited by the Congress prior to the year one thousand eight hundred and eight, but a tax or duty may be imposed on such importation, not exceeding ten dollars for each person.

The privilege of the writ of habeas corpus shall not be suspended, unless when in cases of rebellion or invasion the public safety may require it.

No bill of attainder or ex post facto law shall be passed.

No capitation, [or other direct,] tax shall be laid, unless in proportion to the census or enumeration herein before directed to be taken.

No tax or duty shall be laid on articles exported from any state.

No preference shall be given by any regulation of commerce or revenue to the ports of one state over those of another: nor shall vessels bound to, or from, one state, be obliged to enter, clear or pay duties in another.

No money shall be drawn from the treasury, but in consequence of appropriations made by law; and a regular statement and account of receipts and expenditures of all public money shall be published from time to time.

No title of nobility shall be granted by the United States: and no person holding any office of profit or trust under them, shall, without the consent of the Congress, accept of any present, emolument, office, or title, of any kind whatever, from any king, prince, or foreign state.

Powers Forbidden to the States

Section 10. No state shall enter into any treaty, alliance, or confederation; grant letters of marque and reprisal; coin money; emit bills of credit; make anything but gold and silver coin a tender in payment of debts; pass any bill of attainder, ex post facto law, or law impairing the obligation of contracts, or grant any title of nobility.

No state shall, without the consent of the Congress, lay any imposts or duties on imports or exports, except what may be absolutely necessary for executing its inspection laws: and the net produce of all duties and imposts, laid by any state on imports or exports, shall be for the use of the treasury of the United States; and all such laws shall be subject to the revision and control of the Congress.

No state shall, without the consent of Congress, lay any duty of tonnage, keep troops, or ships of war in time of peace, enter into any agreement or compact with another state, or with a foreign power, or engage in war, unless actually invaded, or in such imminent danger as will not admit of delay.

Article II
The Executive Branch

Section 1. The executive power shall be vested in a President of the United States of America. He shall hold his office during the term of four years, and, together with the Vice President, chosen for the same term, be elected, as follows:

Each state shall appoint, in such manner as the legislature thereof may direct, a number of electors, equal to the whole number of Senators and Representatives to which the State may be entitled in the Congress: but no Senator or Representative, or person holding an office of trust or profit under the United States, shall be appointed an elector.

[The electors shall meet in their respective states, and vote by ballot for two persons, of whom one at least shall not be an inhabitant of the same state with themselves. And they shall make a list of all the persons voted for, and of the number of votes for each; which list they shall sign and certify, and transmit sealed to the seat of the government of the United States, directed to the President of the Senate. The President of the Senate shall, in the presence of the Senate and House of Representatives, open all the certificates, and the votes shall then be counted. The person having the greatest number of votes shall be the President, if such number be a majority of the whole number of electors appointed; and if there be more than one who have such majority, and have an equal number of votes, then the House of Representatives shall immediately choose by ballot one of them for President; and if no person have a majority, then from the five highest on the list the said House shall in like manner choose the President. But in choosing the President, the votes shall be taken by States, the representation from each state having one vote; A quorum for this purpose shall consist of a member or members from two thirds of the states, and a majority of all the states shall be necessary to a choice. In every case, after the choice of the President, the person having the greatest number of votes of the electors shall be the Vice President. But if there should remain two or more who have equal votes, the Senate shall choose from them by ballot the Vice President.]

The Congress may determine the time of choosing the electors, and the day on which they shall give their votes; which day shall be the same throughout the United States.

No person except a natural born citizen, or a citizen of the United States, at the time of the adoption of this Constitution, shall be eligible to the office of President; neither shall any person be eligible to that office who shall not have attained to the age of thirty-five years, and been fourteen Years a resident within the United States.

In case of the removal of the President from office, or of his death, resignation, or inability to discharge the powers and duties of the said office, the same shall devolve on the Vice President, and the Congress may by law provide for the case of removal, death, resignation or inability, both of the President and Vice President, declaring what officer shall then act as President, and such officer shall act accordingly, until the disability be removed, or a President shall be elected.

The President shall, at stated times, receive for his services, a compensation, which shall neither be increased nor diminished during the period for which he shall have been elected, and he shall not receive within that period any other emolument from the United States, or any of them.

Before he enter on the execution of his office, he shall take the following oath or affirmation:—"I do solemnly swear (or affirm) that I will faithfully execute the office of President of the United States, and will to the best of my ability, preserve, protect and defend the Constitution of the United States."

Section 2. The President shall be commander-in-chief of the Army and Navy of the United States, and of the militia of the several states, when called into the actual service of the United States; he may require the opinion, in writing, of the principal officer in each of the executive departments, upon any subject relating to the duties of their respective offices, and he shall have power to grant reprieves and pardons for offenses against the United States, except in cases of impeachment.

He shall have power, by and with the advice and consent of the Senate, to make treaties, provided two-thirds of the Senators present concur; and he shall nominate, and by and with the advice and consent of the Senate, shall appoint ambassadors, other public ministers and consuls, judges of the Supreme Court, and all other officers of the United States, whose appointments are not herein otherwise provided for, and which shall be established by law: but the Congress may by law vest the appointment of such inferior officers, as they think proper, in the President alone, in the courts of law, or in the heads of departments.

The President shall have power to fill up all vacancies that may happen during the recess of the Senate, by granting commissions which shall expire at the end of their next session.

Section 3. He shall from time to time give to the Congress information of the state of the union, and recommend to their consideration such measures as he shall judge necessary and expedient; he may, on extraordinary occasions, convene both Houses, or either of them, and in case of disagreement between them, with respect to the time of adjournment, he may adjourn them to such time as he shall think proper; he shall receive ambassadors and other public ministers; he shall take care that the laws be faithfully executed, and shall commission all the officers of the United States.

Section 4. The President, Vice President and all civil officers of the United States, shall be removed from office on impeachment for, and conviction of, treason, bribery, or other high crimes and misdemeanors.

Article III
The Judicial Branch

Section 1. The judicial power of the United States, shall be vested in one Supreme Court, and in such inferior courts as the Congress may from time to time ordain and establish. The judges, both of the supreme and inferior courts, shall hold their offices during good behaviour, and shall, at stated times, receive for their services, a compensation, which shall not be diminished during their continuance in office.

Section 2. The judicial power shall extend to all cases, in law and equity, arising under this Constitution, the laws of the United States, and treaties made, or which shall be made, under their authority;—to all cases affecting ambassadors, other public ministers and consuls;—to all cases of admiralty and maritime jurisdiction, [—to controversies to which the United States shall be a party;—to controversies between two or more states, [between a state and citizens of another state;], between citizens of different states;—between citizens of the same state, claiming lands under grants of different states, and between a state, or the citizens thereof, and foreign states, [citizens or subjects].

In all cases affecting ambassadors, other public ministers and consuls, and those in which a state shall be party, the Supreme Court shall have original jurisdiction. In all the other cases before mentioned, the Supreme Court shall have appellate jurisdiction, both as to law and fact, with such exceptions, and under such regulations as the Congress shall make.

The trial of all crimes, except in cases of impeach-ment, shall be by jury; and such trial shall be held in the state where the said crimes shall have been committed; but when not committed within any state, the trial shall be at such place or places as the Congress may by law have directed.

Section 3. Treason against the United States, shall consist only in levying war against them, or in adhering to their enemies, giving them aid and comfort. No person shall be convicted of treason unless on the testimony of two witnesses to the same overt act, or on confession in open court.

The Congress shall have power to declare the punishment of treason, but no attainder of treason shall work corruption of blood, or forfeiture except during the life of the person attainted.

Article IV
Relation of the States to Each Other

Section 1. Full faith and credit shall be given in each state to the public acts, records, and judicial proceedings of every other state. And the Congress may by general laws prescribe the manner in which such acts, records, and proceedings shall be proved, and the effect thereof.

Section 2. The citizens of each state shall be entitled to all privileges and immunities of citizens in the several states.

A person charged in any state with treason, felony, or other crime, who shall flee from justice, and be found in another state, shall on demand of the executive authority of the state from which he fled, be delivered up, to be removed to the state having jurisdiction of the crime.

[No person held to service or labor in one state, under the laws thereof, escaping into another, shall, in consequence of any law or regulation therein, be discharged from such service or labor, but shall be delivered up on claim of the party to whom such service or labor may be due.]

Federal-State Relations

Section 3. New states may be admitted by the Congress into this Union; but no new states shall be formed or erected within the jurisdiction of any other state, nor any state be formed by the junction of two or more states, without the consent of the legislatures of the states concerned, as well as of the Congress.

The Congress shall have power to dispose of and make all needful rules and regulations respecting the territory or other property belonging to the United States; and nothing in this Constitution shall be so construed as to prejudice any claims of the United States, or of any particular state.

Section 4. The United States shall guarantee to every state in this union a republican form of government, and shall protect each of them against invasion; and on application of the legislature, or of the executive (when the legislature cannot be convened) against domestic violence.

Article V
Amending the Constitution

The Congress, whenever two thirds of both houses shall deem it necessary, shall propose amendments to this Constitution, or, on the application of the legislatures of two thirds of the several states, shall call a convention for proposing amendments, which, in either case, shall be valid to all intents and purposes, as part of this Constitution, when ratified by the legislatures of three fourths of the several states, or by conventions in three fourths thereof, as the one or the other mode of ratification may be proposed by the Congress; provided [that no amendment which may be made prior to the year one thousand eight hundred and eight shall in any manner affect the first and fourth clauses in the ninth section of the first article; and] that no state, without its consent, shall be deprived of its equal suffrage in the Senate.

Article VI
National Debts

All debts contracted and engagements entered into, before the adoption of this Constitution, shall be as valid against the United States under this Constitution, as under the Confederation.

Supremacy of the National Government

This Constitution, and the laws of the United States which shall be made in pursuance thereof; and all treaties made, or which shall be made, under the authority of the United States, shall be the supreme law of the land; and the judges in every state shall be bound thereby, anything in the constitution or laws of any State to the contrary notwithstanding.

The senators and representatives before mentioned, and the members of the several state legislatures, and all executive and judicial officers, both of the United States and of the several states, shall be bound by oath or affirmation, to support this Constitution; but no religious test shall ever be required as a qualification to any office or public trust under the United States.

Article VII
Ratifying the Constitution

The ratification of the conventions of nine states, shall be sufficient for the establishment of this Constitution between the states so ratifying the same.

Done in convention by the unanimous consent of the states present the seventeenth day of September in the year of our Lord one thousand seven hundred and eighty seven and of the independence of the United States of America the twelfth. In witness whereof we have hereunto subscribed our Names.

Amendment II

A well regulated Militia, being necessary to the security of a free State, the right of the people to keep and bear Arms, shall not be infringed.

Report Links

The Internet sites described below can be accessed at http://www.myreportlinks.com

▶**The Charters of Freedom: Bill of Rights**
Editor's Choice Travel back to the founding of the nation with digital scans of these important documents.

▶**Second Amendment Research Center**
Editor's Choice Explore scholarship on the Second Amendment.

▶**Justice Learning: Gun Control**
Editor's Choice Explore opposing views on the Second Amendment.

▶**Documents From the Continental Congress and the Constitutional Convention**
Editor's Choice See clean copies of documents circulated at the Constitutional Convention.

▶**Brady Campaign to Prevent Gun Violence**
Editor's Choice Learn about the group that supported the Brady Bill to ban assault weapons.

▶**Second Amendment Foundation**
Editor's Choice See how the Second Amendment is interpreted in each state's constitution.

▶**America During the Age of Revolution, 1764–1775**
Travel through time and see the events of the American Revolution.

▶**American Civil Liberties Union: Gun Control**
What does the ACLU think about issues of gun control/gun rights?

▶**The American Revolution: Lighting Freedom's Flame**
Learn about the important battles of the American Revolution.

▶**The Anti-Federalist Papers**
Read some opposing views of the Constitution.

▶**Army National Guard: History**
Learn about the Army National Guard, which dates back to colonial times.

▶**Ben's Guide to U.S. Government**
Discover basic information about how the government operates, for young people at all levels of study.

▶**The Coalition to Stop Gun Violence**
Find news, research, and advocacy from a group that seeks to lessen gun violence.

▶***The Federalist:* A Collection of Essays**
Read the famous papers written to support the Constitution.

▶**FindLaw: U.S. Constitution: Second Amendment**
See the writings that lawyers consider in Second Amendment cases.

Report Links

The Internet sites described below can be accessed at
http://www.myreportlinks.com

▶**Firearms Program: Bureau of Alcohol, Tobacco, Firearms & Explosives**
Learn about the federal government's regulation of firearms.

▶*The Founders' Constitution*
Read firsthand accounts of thinking on constitutional issues from centuries past.

▶**Gun Guys: Where Everyone's a Straight Shooter**
Views of current events about gun rights, from a group that wants greater gun control.

▶*Guns & Ammo:* **2nd Amendment**
Practical information for gun owners from a leading gun enthusiast magazine.

▶**Johns Hopkins Bloomberg School of Public Health: Center for Gun Policy and Research**
This center looks at gun violence as a public health issue.

▶*Liberty! The American Revolution*
Get a feel for the people and times of the American Revolution.

▶**Million Mom March**
The Million Mom March is a group with the objectives of "sensible gun laws, safe kids."

▶**Minuteman Project**
See the parallels of the Minuteman Project to the militias of centuries past.

▶**National Park Service: Boston National Historical Park**
See the evidence of some of the important battles in the American Revolution.

▶**National Rifle Association**
Read about the nation's largest group for gun owners.

▶**National Rifle Association: Safety Programs—Eddie Eagle**
Decide whether the NRA's Eddie Eagle program for young people sends a positive message.

▶**North Carolina Citizen Militia**
Learn about a group that finds its inspiration in the militias of centuries past.

▶**Southern Poverty Law Center: Intelligence Project**
Determine if there are ties between modern militias and racially motivated hate groups.

▶**The Supreme Court Historical Society**
Learn all about the history of the Supreme Court.

▶**Supreme Court of the United States**
See how the Supreme Court works, and meet the justices.

boycott—Refuse to do or use something as a means of protest.

dismissed—A judge may dismiss, or throw away, a court case if he or she believes there is not enough evidence to support the charge.

eastern seaboard—All of the states along the Atlantic coast of the United States.

encroachment—The act of infringing upon the belongings, rights, or territories of a person or group.

endorsement—Support. If you are running for school president and receive an endorsement from the town Recreation Center, it means the center is on your side. They believe that you are the best candidate for president.

deserters—People who leave a group or place with the intention of never returning again.

House of Representatives—One of the two houses of the United States Congress. The Senate is the other house. Each state, depending on their population size, has a certain number of individual who act as their state representatives.

indicted—When a person is indicted, it means that he or she has been accused of a crime or wrongdoing.

infringe—Violate or disobey. Someone who infringes upon a law has broken the law.

jurisdiction—The power of a court to hear and decide a case.

ordained—The Constitution was ordained, or intended for, the people of the United States. Its creation was not meant for anyone else.

Parliament—A ruling body that meets to discuss and make laws. Parliament has the ultimate power when it comes to making laws.

prohibit—Forbid the use of something. A sign that reads "Running is Prohibited in hallways" means that running is not allowed.

ratify—Legally approve something. When Congress ratifies a law, they agree with, and support, everything that the law says.

regulate—Manage or rule. When someone regulates a law or project, he or she makes sure that things are run according to the rules.

repeal—Remove a law. The courts have the power to use this action. A court usually repeals a law or act if they believe it has negative consequences for society or if they believe it is no longer useful.

unanimous—If every vote that has been entered says yes to school uniforms, the vote is unanimous. Everyone agrees.

unconstitutional—Not in keeping with the wording of the U.S. Constitution.

Chapter 1. The Second Amendment Today

1. Press Release from County of Sonoma District Attorney, "Homicide Ruled Justifiable in Healdsburg Home Invasion," *County of Sonoma District Attorney,* May 2, 2006, <http://www.sonoma-county.org/Da/press_releases/press_050206.htm> (October 27, 2006).

2. "WISQARS Injury Mortality Reports 1999–2003," *National Center for Injury Prevention and Control,* n.d., <http://webapp.cdc.gov/cgi-bin/broker.exe> (October 27, 2006).

3. "Statistics: Gun Violence in Our Communities," *National Education Association: Health Information Network,* April 14, 2005, <http://www.neahin.org/programs/schoolsafety/gunsafety/statistics.htm#children> (October 27, 2006).

4. Ibid.

5. "Crimes Committed with Firearms, 1973–2004," *U.S. Department of Justice, Office of Justice Programs,* September 25, 2006, <www.ojp.usdoj.gov/bjs/glance/tables/guncrimetab.htm> (October 27, 2006).

Chapter 2. The History of the Second Amendment

1. Kris E. Palmer, *Constitutional Amendments: 1789 to the Present* (Detroit: Gale Group Inc., 2000), p. 41.

2. Ibid, p. 45.

3. Keith A. Ehrman and Dennis A. Henigan, "The Second Amendment in the Twentieth Century: Have You Seen Your Militia Lately?" *The Legal Action Project,* n.d., Reprinted from University of Dayton Law Review, vol. 15, No. 1, Fall 1989, <www.gunlawsuits.org/defend/second/articles/twentieth.php> (October 27, 2006).

4. Palmer, p. 45.

5. Ehrman and Henigan.

Chapter 3. Individual or Collective Right?

1. Wayne LaPierre, *Guns, Freedom, and Terrorism* (Nashville, Tennessee: Thomas Nelson, Inc., 2003), p. 31.

2. Lee Epstein and Thomas G. Walker, *Constitutional Law For a Changing America* (Washington, D.C.: CQ Press, 2001), p. 404.

3. Robert L. Maddex, *The U.S. Constitution A to Z* (Washington, D.C.: CQ Press, 2002), p. 227.

Chapter 4. The Second Amendment in Court: 1785–1960

1. Kris E. Palmer, *Constitutional Amendments: 1789 to the Present* (Detroit: Gale Group Inc., 2000), p. 46.

2. "Amendment II, Document 8, *Bliss* v. *Commonwealth*", *The Founders' Constitution,* n.d., <http://press-pubs.uchicago.edu/founders/documents/amendIIs8.html> (October 27, 2006).

3. *"Barron* v. *Mayor & City of Baltimore,* 32 U.S. 243 (1833)", *The Constitution Society,* n.d., <www.constitution.org/ussc/032-243a.htm> (October 27, 2006).

4. Ibid.

5. Palmer, p. 47.

6. *"Nunn* v. *State* 1 Kelly 243 (Ga. 1846)", *NFA and Other Gun Law Related Info and Cases,* n.d., <http://www.cs.cmu.edu/afs/cs/user/wbardwel/public/nfalist/nunn_v_state.txt> (October 30, 2006).

7. *"U.S.* v. *Cruikshank,* 92 U.S. 542 (1875)", *FindLaw for Legal Professionals,* n.d., <http://caselaw.lp.findlaw.com/scripts/getcase.pl?navby=case&court=us&vol=92&page=542> (October 30, 2006).

8. Palmer, p. 51.

9. *"U.S.* v. *Miller,* 307 U.S. 174 (1939)", *NFA and Other Gun Law Related Info and Cases,* n.d., <http://www.cs.cmu.edu/afs/cs/user/wbardwel/public/nfalist/miller.txt> (October 30, 2006).

10. Ibid.

11. Keith A. Ehrman and Dennis A. Henigan, "The Second Amendment in the Twentieth Century: Have You Seen Your Militia Lately?" *The Legal Action Project,*

n.d., Reprinted from *University of Dayton Law Review,* vol. 15, No. 1, Fall 1989, <www.gunlawsuits.org/ defend/second/articles/twentieth.php> (October 27, 2006).

12. *U.S.* v. *Miller.*

13. Lee Epstein and Thomas G. Walker, *Constitutional Law For A Changing America* (Washington, D.C.: CQ Press, 2001), p. 406.

14. Wayne LaPierre and James Jay Baker, *Shooting Straight: Telling the Truth About Guns In America* (Washington, D.C.: Regnery Publishing, Inc., 2002), p. 109.

15. *U.S.* v. *Miller.*

16. Henry J. Abraham and Barbara A. Perry, *Freedom and the Court: Civil Rights and Liberties in the United States,* 8th ed. (Lawrence: University Press of Kansas, 2003), pp. 102–103.

17. "*Cases* v. *U.S.,* 131 F.2d 916 (1st Cir. 1942)," *NFA and Other Gun Law Related Info and Cases,* n.d., <www.cs.cmu.edu/afs/cs/usr/wbardwel/public/ nfalist/cases_v_us.txt> (October 30, 2006).

18. Ibid.

Chapter 5. The Second Amendment in Court: 1960–Present

1. "*Burton* v. *Sills,* 53 N.J. 86 (1968)", *NFA and Other Gun Law Related Info and Cases,* n.d., <www.cs.cmu.edu/afs/cs/usr/wbardwel/public/nfalist/ burton_v_sills.txt> (October 30, 2006).

2. Lee Epstein and Thomas G. Walker, *Constitutional Law For A Changing America* (Washington, D.C.: CQ Press, 2001), p. 406.

3. Henry J. Abraham and Barbara A. Perry, *Freedom and the Court: Civil Rights and Liberties in the United States,* 8th ed. (Lawrence: University Press of Kansas, 2003), p. 102.

4. "The Assault Weapons Ban: Frequently Asked Questions," *Brady Campaign To Prevent Gun Violence,* n.d., <www.bradycampaign.org/facts/faqs/?page= awb> (October 30, 2006).

5. Supreme Court Collection, *"United States* v. *Lopez* (93-1260), 514 U.S. 549 (1995)", *Cornell Law School,* n.d., <http://supct.law.cornell.edu/supct/ html/93-1260.ZC1.html> (October 30, 2006).

6. "ASK Campaign: Statistics," *PAX: Real solutions to Gun Violence,* n.d., <http://www.paxusa.org/ask/ statistics.html>, (October 30, 2006).

7. Donna Dees-Thomases with Alison Hendrie, *Looking For A Few Good Moms: How One Mother Rallied A Million Others Against the Gun Lobby* (Pennsylvania: Rodale Inc., 2004), p. 226.

8. *"Kitchen* v. *K-Mart Corp.,* 697 So.2d 1200 (Fla.1997)", *NFA and Other Gun Law Related Info and Cases,* n.d., <http://www.cs.cmu.edu/afs/cs/usr/ wbardwel/public/nfalist/kitchen_v_k_mart.txt> (October 30, 2006).

9. *City of Chicago* v. *Beretta U.S.A. Corp,* 821 N.E. 2nd 1099 (Ill. 2004).

10. U.S. District Court of Northern District of Texas San Angelo Division, "Criminal Action No. 6: 98-CR-103-C," *U.S.* v. *Emerson,* 1999, <http://lw.bna.com/ lw/19990504/698.htm> (October 30, 2006).

11. "Crimes Committed with Firearms, 1973–2004," *U.S. Department of Justice, Office of Justice Programs,* September 25, 2006, <www.ojp.usdoj.gov /bjs/glance/tables/guncrimetab.htm> (October 27, 2006).

Chapter 6. The Future of the Second Amendment

1. Lee Epstein and Thomas G. Walker, *Constitutional Law For A Changing America* (Washington, D.C.: CQ Press, 2001), p. 406.

2. Henry J. Abraham and Barbara A. Perry, *Freedom and the Court: Civil Rights and Liberties in the United States,* 8th ed., (Kansas: University Press of Kansas, 2003), p. 103.

3. Wayne LaPierre and James Jay Baker, *Shooting Straight: Telling the Truth About Guns In America* (Washington, D.C., Regnery Publishing, Inc., 2002), p. 112.

4. Epstein and Walker, p. 403.

5. Robert L. Maddex, *The U.S. Constitution A to Z* (Washington, D.C.: CQ Press, 2002), p. 227.

6. "Crimes Committed with Firearms, 1973-2004," U.S. Department of Justice, Office of Justice Programs, September 25, 2006, <www.ojp.usdoj.gov/bjs/glance/tables/guncrimetab.htm> (October 27, 2006).

7. LaPierre and Baker, p. 31.

8. Loren Berger and Dennis Henigan, *Guns and Terror* (Washington, D.C.: Brady Center to Prevent Gun Violence, 2001), p. 3.

Crooker, Constance Emerson. *Gun Control and Gun Rights*. Westpoint, Conn.: Greenwood Press, 2003.

Freedman, Russell. *In Defense of Liberty: the Story of America's Bill of Rights*. New York: Holiday House, 2003.

Green, Carl R. *The War of 1812*. Berkeley Heights, N.J.: MyReportlinks.com Books, 2002.

Hurley, Jennifer A. *The 1960s*. San Diego, Calif.: Greenhaven Press, 2000.

Katcher, Philip. *Sharpshooters of the Civil War.* Chicago, Ill.: Raintree, 2003.

Kent, Zachary. *James Madison: Creating a Nation*. Berkeley Heights, N.J.: Enslow Publishers, 2004.

Kraft, Betsey Harvey. *Theodore Roosevelt: Champion of the American Spirit*. New York: Clarion Books, 2003.

Maestro, Betsy. *Liberty or Death: The American Revolution, 1763–1783*. New York: HarperCollins, 2005.

McClung, Robert M. *Young George Washington and the French and Indian Wars: 1753-1758.* New Haven, Conn.: Linnet Books, 2002.

Payan, Gregory. *The Federalists and Anti-federalists: How and Why Political Parties Were Formed in Young America*. New York: Rosen Pub. Company, 2004.

Raatma, Lucia. *The Minutemen*. Minneapolis, Minn.: Compass Point Books, 2005.

Spitzer, Robert J. *The Right to Bear Arms: Rights and Liberties Under the Law*. Santa Barbara, Calif.: ABC-CLIO, 2001.